Andrew Ings has written many articles for a range of titles for over 20 years. These have included theatrical reviews for a number of newspapers and magazines such as *Arts East, Centre Stage*, the *Jazz Rag* and the *Guardian*. He has also written a number of sketches for the stage and his first book was published in 2001. Andrew has broadcast on the arts, focusing on the theatre in particular, and was a contributor to a weekly radio programme on the arts for more than three years. He currently works freelance for a number of theatres in London. He is also an advisor to the Mountview Academy of Theatrical Arts.

ROCKIN' AT THE 2 I'S COFFEE BAR

Andrew Ings

Book Guild Publishing

Sussex, England

First published in Great Britain in 2010 by
The Book Guild Ltd
Pavilion View
19 New Road
Brighton,
BN1 1UF

Paperback edition 2010

The author and publishers are grateful to all
who have helped with additional research for this book.
Every effort has been made to trace copyright holders,
and we would be pleased to hear from any
we have been unable to reach.

Typeset in Garamond by Ellipsis Books Limited, Glasgow

Printed in Great Britain by CPI Antony Rowe

A catalogue record for this book is available from The British Library.

ISBN 978 1 84624 583 1

Many thanks to my wife Muriel for help with proof reading throughout my work on this book.

Contents

CONTENTS

Preface

In putting this book together I have tried to contact as many people as I could and get their personal memories of an exciting period and community in London's West End.

It is all too easy to forget things, places, tales and memories that do not always register their significance at the time.

These collected items hopefully give an insight into a very important era in the development of British pop music and the area of Little Italy – Soho.

Grateful thanks to all who have contributed including:

Ron Gould – Pip Granger – Micky Ashman – Ron Bowden – Raye Du-Val – Clem Cattini – Joe Moretti – Russ Sainty – Gerry Champion – Lynn Terry – Howard Tibble – Chas McDevitt – Tony Annis – Michael Fogerty – Betty Osmont – Sir Cliff Richard – Big Jim Sullivan – Danny Rivers – John Pilgrim – Hylda Simms – Dave Samson – Wee Willie Harris – Bob Jackson – Terry Dene – Jean Heath – John D'Avensac – Dorothy Hardy – Clive Stuart – Christine Runicles – Ed Pearson – Brian 'Liquorice' Locking – Vince Eager – Jay Chance – Vince Raynor – Julie Samuel – Christine Ford – Eric Nugent – Peter Mole – Terry Wayne – Pauline Webber – John Harris – Gordon Fleming.

Also Bill Haynes and Ken Major

And thanks to Keith Woods of *Tales From The Woods* for his help and support.

Tales From The Woods is an off-the-wall roots music magazine, reflecting the music, humour and occasionally the politics of the contributors and editor.

It also incorporates theatre and cinema as well as a jazz column and the more contemporary sounds are catered for via a regular and popular column within the publication.

And special thanks to my wife Muriel who has proofread and corrected my errors.

Foreword by Keith Woods

I can truly say, without fear of contradiction or exaggeration, that I was there; perhaps even a party to this book's conception that took place upon the hallowed floor of the legendary 100 Club in Oxford street, London, on the bitterly cold last Sunday in January 2007. I am sure that my good friend Andrew Ings would not disagree.

Maybe the idea of this book had been swimming around in the author's head for months, possibly years before, but it was at this Tribute to the 2 I's show that the embryonic idea developed, with Andrew taking me to one side during the course of this hectic, exciting, and sometimes a little chaotic, evening.

'Keith, there just has to be a book about these people, and nobody has written it yet.' Indeed nobody had.

The book is devoted entirely to what was very much a London based phenomenon, and of course the tiny basement coffee bar venue in Old Compton Street, Soho, the 2 I's.

Without its existence, there may not have been the multi-billion pound music industry that is now taken for granted, encompassing the numerous other clubs and coffee bars that lined the streets of 1950s Soho and the surrounding area, whose names cannot fail to bring a smile to even the most forlorn face, or to have an exotic ring of history to those long from being born. I'm talking about the Top Ten Club, the Freight Train, Bread Basket, and Cy Laurie's Jazz Club, to name just a few.

It brings together so many of the original artists, musicians and fans whose memories will unfold before your eyes as you turn the pages of this encyclopedia of anecdotes from those who were there at the time.

The venues may have long passed into history, but they live on in these pages to tell their stories to those who wish to remember, as well as to future generations, who through these pages can live through such an essential piece of musical history. The birth of British rock 'n' roll, evolved from Skiffle, which in turn came from the post-war boom in New Orleans Jazz.

Through the eyes and the words of the characters that strode the streets of 1950s Soho, we see perhaps the optimism that would mushroom so famously in the decade that would follow and, in the opinion of many, unfairly overshadow the 1950s.

I have no doubt in my mind that many of the artists and musicians, whose words flow so effortlessly through these pages, could have been much bigger stars than they actually became, had those that managed them and guided their careers, both inside and outside the recording studio, had the benefit of hindsight, or even just a slice of the understanding that their 1960s contemporaries displayed.

When the Tribute to the 2 I's show was over, the song set lists were folded away for posterity, and photographs of this historic evening carefully indexed and placed in boxes.

Soon the phone was ringing, Andrew was up and running, ready to get this book on the road, meeting many contributors at the private upstairs bar of a West London pub, famous for housing a folk club for almost as many years as are covered within these pages. It is however maybe more famous for many of you as being just yards from where the Bread Basket Coffee Bar once stood.

I am sure Andrew would not disagree that in so many cases we simply let the tape roll. There was little prompting required in recounting stories of a life lived through those early glory days, often told with enthusiasm and devotion like they were being told for the first time. Nor was there any sign of a weary gaze or disinterested tone that would suggest the thought of 'not those days again'.

It was great fun, and I feel privileged to sit with these revered names of early British rock 'n' roll and our own home-grown alternative, Skiffle.

I must just mention one important person. At some point during the autumn of 2005, as the first tentative steps were being taken towards presenting a celebration of fifty years of Skiffle (to be held the following January at a King's Cross venue, London) one of the first people I would contact would be the wonderful Rick Hardy. He would prove invaluable to this club promoter, providing names, contact addresses, telephone numbers, and of course a million and one anecdotes. Rick, one time leader of the Rick Richards' Skiffle Group, was up and raring to go, with energy and enthusiasm as if it was being done for the very first time.

Original members of the group, Johnny D'Avensac and Tex Makins, were called on to drop whatever they were doing and play it again, one more time, for a celebration of this uniquely British musical form.

We became good friends and Rick was soon showing the same forthright eagerness to be involved in the plans for the aforementioned Tribute to the 2 I's gig.

Just a couple of weeks away from Christmas 2006, we held a celebratory Christmas party at the Fitzrovia pub in Goodge Street, where so many of the interviews for this book took place.

Rick performed for us on that gloriously happy and memorable evening, as did his near lifelong friend Chas McDevitt, and several other veteran 2 I's performers. Rick however, had more claim to this world-famous cellar bar than most, as Rick was, for over eighteen months, the venue's resident performer.

Barely more than twenty-four hours later, while driving home from a gig in Brentford, south-west London, Rick was involved in a head-on collision with a vehicle driven by a drunk driver, tragically dying from his injuries a couple of hours later, deprived of the opportunity to perform at the celebration of the tiny basement club that was so close to his heart.

Just months before, Rick, along with so many of the other artists and musicians, spent a warm, sunny afternoon being entertained by the present owners of the establishment amidst the glare of the media, when the City of Westminster council placed a plaque on the wall outside the building where the 2 I's once had its home. The January performance that he was so looking forward to was dedicated to his memory.

There can be no doubt that Rick would have been overjoyed that a book has finally been written chronicling the place where he had performed for so long and where he looked back with so much fondness.

If like me, you were just a child when the 2 I's, Freight Train, Bread Basket and other venues were all at their peak, no doubt all sorts of half-faded memories will find their way into your consciousness.

Once again, Uncle Sidney will be rolling around the floor in helpless laughter at the antics of Jimmy Edwards and Dick Bentley on the BBC light programme *Take It From Here*. As a child you would be curled up in an armchair, mouth agape at the exploits of Jet Morgan and his crew stepping on to the surface of Mars in *Journey Into Space*, while upstairs your big sister would be in her bedroom. A needle touches down on a shiny surface, a slightly nasal voice rings out in a mid-Atlantic accent: 'Now this is the story of the Rock Island Line . . .'

Unbeknown to all of us, history was in the making.

Keith Woods © 2008

Soho – A Brief History and Picture

The area we call Soho has been known as such for around 400 years. Back in the early Middle Ages it was grazing and marsh land. Even as recently as the early part of the twentieth century there were flooding and drainage problems. Mind you, looking at recent happenings in this country, this is nothing new.

The name Soho is thought to have been the original hunting cry 'SO-HOE' when this part of London was used by the gentry of the period, before settlers began to move in and develop the area. The locality was taken over by Henry VIII as a royal park. It is recorded that 'SO-HOE' was also a rallying call for the soldiers at the Battle of Sedgmoor in 1685.

Towards the end of the seventeenth century the crown granted Soho fields to Henry Jermyn, the first Earl of St. Albans. He let out most of the area to one man, Joseph Girle, who planned to start building with Richard Frith. From him comes the name Frith Street, which rose to fame when John Logie Baird gave the world the first demonstration of television in January 1926.

To commemorate this there is a plaque above the Bar Italia at 22 Frith Street. This place has been an all-night Soho favourite since 1923. The bar serves great Italian coffee and it is absolutely packed whenever there is a televised Italian football match. In the same street there is a plaque above the stage door of the Prince Edward Theatre which identifies the site where Mozart lived for a few years as a child.

Inevitably the character of the area changed over time, on the one hand partly from neglect by those with money, hence its lack of development, and on the other from the influence of the newcomers with a multitude of culture and customs. The big money went to the redevelopment of other areas in central London.

The area in general and Old Compton Street in particular became populated by French refugees after Charles II gave protection to of flats in Soho. In all, the street is home to more than thirty restaurants and bars.

The name 'Little Italy' did not happen by chance. These days we are familiar with Italian dishes but several generations ago; if you wanted real Parmigiano cheese, for instance, you had to trail into Old Compton Street to get it. This street was named after Henry Compton, who raised funds for a local parish church, eventually dedicated as St. Anne's Church in 1686. The spire of St. Anne's Church was designed by John Meard, a developer after whom Meard Street is named. Past residents of Old Compton Street have included a royal physician and a couple of servants to Queen Anne.

By the end of the nineteenth century the Italians were forming political units in clubs such as the Mazzini Garibaldi, which was in Red Lion Square. It was an important venue from its establishment in 1864 until it closed in 2008.

These fascist clubs provided more of a social environment than an overtly political one. They were generally ignored by the resident British until the outbreak of the Second World War. As a result of the war many Italian restaurants and delicatessens had their windows smashed. One grocer in Soho even put up a notice saying that they only sold British food and The Spaghetti House restaurant renamed itself the British Food Shop.

Old Compton Street is in fact the 'high street' of Soho and is still at the heart of 'Little Italy'. Some of the original delicatessens are still there including the Lina Stores and I Camisa & Son.

The latter is a delicatessen that imports the best of Italy to the heart of Soho, selling pasta, olive oil, beans, organic Sicilian tomatoes, bread and wine. It has specialities conducive to the time of year such as stocking treats specific to Easter and Christmas, and fresh white truffles when they are in season. The décor has a rustic feel to it, mushrooms hang from the ceiling, and sawdust is scattered along the floor, making the shop all the more appealing.

One of the oldest establishments in Old Compton Street is the Algerian Coffee Stores. It has been here for 120 years and is now run by Paul Crocetta from Naples. The range of coffee available in the shop is amazing.

Old Compton Street had all anyone needed – butcher, baker, grocer, delicatessen, an old lady who sold cheese and a firm called Annello and

David who sold ballet shoes, clothes and accessories. Of course trade came from the theatrical crowd who were in the area very often.

Situated on the corner of Old Compton Street and Dean Street with a conspicuously large ten-foot mannequin perched above the door, Cafe Torino was a favoured haunt for many of the arty sects prevalent in London in the mid 1950s. It was a tiny slice of Soho that stood as a testament to the enduring influence of cafés on the creative life of a Britain emerging from the cultural shell-shock of the Second World War.

Cafés like Torino were very much part of the birth of British cool. Torino regular Dan Farson, in his memoir *Soho In The Fifties* recalled:

Torino's had been run for fourteen years by Mr and Mrs Minella from Italy, together with their son. It was pleasantly old-fashioned with tall, arched windows, and opened at eight-thirty in the morning, closing at seven o'clock in the evening. It had wrought-iron tables with marble tops, cups of proper coffee, and vol-au-vents at one shilling and sixpence. Officially it was a restaurant serving pizza, spaghetti and risotto, but you could talk for hours over a small cup of coffee and the Minellas did not mind. They were so anxious to keep their customers happy they kept their prices low and were rash enough to allow credit. Their goodwill was reciprocated and the tables were usually crowded. There were dark Italians huddled in earnest discussions, suddenly bursting into furious argument . . . and several pale young artists and poets searching half-heartedly for jobs . . .'

Richard Wollheim, reviewing Colin MacInnes' novel *Absolute Beginners* in 1959, insisted the 'hip' coffee bar kids of the 1950s represented an aristocracy of 'cool' whose dominion he specifically located in 'films from France, Poland and Japan and in the cafés and bars of every American or Americanized city in the world.'

At the end of Old Compton Street, where it meets Charing Cross Road, was one of the best cafés in Soho in 1954. On the right was the Star Restaurant, which was more of a 'greasy spoon'. It was run by a very friendly Greek known as Andreas, with a couple of part-time waiters at the weekend. The décor was spartan at best with Rexine tablecloths and simple wooden furniture. The toilets were in an alley that led directly onto the street, handy if you were taken short and had no money. The menu was chips-with-everything, with nothing remotely Greek on offer. You could get two sausages with chunky chips, a slice of bread and butter and a tea for less than two shillings.

As well as hip teens, the cafés, pubs and drinking clubs attracted many of London's leading intellectuals and artists of the time, including the scions of Soho, Francis Bacon, John Minton, Lucien Freud, Henrietta Moraes and Frank Auerbach.

'London in the fifties was a Mecca for artists', the painter Jack Smith declared, 'The wilderness starts ten miles from the centre of London in any direction.'

In those days when you walked down the few streets that made up Soho you could hear all kinds of music coming from the different venues. Sadly today it is not the case, and for that you can blame the government and local licensing laws – and heaven forbid 'elf and safety.

Right at the far end of Old Compton Street, next to the Coach & Horses pub was a dingy café called The French. Here a character called Iron Foot Jack used to hold forth. Iron Foot Jack – Jack Nieve – was a notorious tramp and created for himself the title and self-styled image of 'King of the Bohemians'. He was overweight, bald on top and had long white hair. He wore a homburg hat and often had a long black cape slung over his shorter leg, which was elevated by an iron boot. This had a steel plate on the bottom and when he was drunk – which was frequently – he used to drag his foot, which created lots of sparks as it caught the pavement. He was also known to jump on to the bonnets and roofs of cars, causing a lot of damage. He would also approach the unwary and try to sell them copies of his poems on pieces of grubby paper.

Jack had very poor personal hygiene – so he always could be seen sitting alone in various cafés.

The Bohemian underworlds of Fitzrovia and Soho were a magnet for all kinds of eccentrics, artists, musicians and actors. Painter Francis Bacon became the most famous member of the circle centred on the legendary Colony Room in Soho, run by Muriel Belcher, a drinking den frequented by artists, critics and assorted hangers-on. Bacon was, in fact, a founding member, walking in the day after it opened in 1948. He was allowed free drinks and £10 a week to bring in friends and rich patrons. Among the regulars was George Melly who actually met his wife there.

The city was brimming over with ideas and movements: Neo-Romanticism, Social Realism, Pop Art, the Kitchen Sink School, Abstract Expressionism all jostled with each other for dominance.

London, and Soho in particular, in the 1950s, with all its vigour and fertility was a city in the midst of intellectual and artistic ferment.

It is perhaps no coincidence that towards the end of the 1950s with the Cold War firmly established, and the Soviet bloc making 'the bomb', that maybe some thought World War III was going to happen. So to hell with it – let's live for today.

Drugs were – according to old tales – readily available from US servicemen over here who would drive into the West End, park their cars in Wardour Street and sell their goods.

Ron Gould (from the Southern Skiffle Group and The Vipers) remembered a trumpeter in the mid 1950s called Jimmy Fox, who was the first person Ron had ever seen smoking marijuana. Later, in 1959, when he was touring Ireland with John Pilgrim and The Vipers they came across a tobacconist called James Fox – Tobacco Blenders!

One specific memory of the drug scene I have received is from Lynn Terry who told me, 'I think it was in early 1961 that I was aware of cannabis being smoked by the musicians but not before that. It probably was available but not to my knowledge'. More from Lynn later.

The first recorded UK arrest for cannabis was at Club Eleven in 1952. It was located at 41 Great Windmill Street and is generally revered as the fountainhead of modern jazz in Britain.

Club Eleven, named after the number of founder members, began life just before Christmas in 1948. It was a co-operative arrangement designed to bring bebop to the attention of the jazz public at large. The musicians involved included Ronnie Scott, Tony Crombie and Laurie Morgan, plus manager Harry Morris. Johnny Dankworth and Denis Rose were regulars from the start. This venue with these musicians was home to the first truly organized bebop sessions in Britain. With the star-studded assembly of musicians, Club Eleven became the focal point for the new jazz and the inspiration to many other young musicians throughout the country.

2 I's Coffee Bar

It was by pure chance that I was walking through Soho one lunchtime in September 2006. Turning the corner from Wardour Street into Old Compton Street I was confronted by the obvious excitement of a small crowd of people, cameras and other media.

My first reaction was that they were shooting a scene for yet another soap opera – so I continued in my pursuit of a sandwich and a glass of wine. After all, it was lunchtime.

Later I emerged from lunch to find the crowd had been joined by some very elegant and mature-looking teddy boys. They really looked terrific in 'ted's' gear, and my curiosity was aroused, especially as I can remember that era well.

Their response to my questions was that a plaque commemorating the 2 I's coffee bar was about to be unveiled.

Ah! the 2 I's coffee bar – that really began to stir up my memory bank and with that my plans for the afternoon were suspended. I ended up in the Compton Arms talking at great length to several old rockers.

Although there were many coffee bars around the area the 2 I's and a bar called the Skiffle Cellar were major venues with only a few steps between them.

The 2 I's was at 59 Old Compton Street and the Skiffle Cellar was at 49 Greek Street – both great places but they attracted very different crowds.

The specific row of property in which the 2 I's stood was originally built in the early eighteenth century by Owen Sainsbury. It survived – only just – a bombing raid during the Second World War.

Now the Boulevard Bar/Restaurant, the 2 I's was the smaller of the two and sold coffee at street level with all the action happening down in the basement.

In 1958 the 2 I's was the fuse for the explosion that was to come in the world of British rock 'n' roll.

Before Cliff Richard, there was a major happening in music called 'Skiffle', and there were various Skiffle bands. Some of them had hits in the charts, such as the great Lonnie Donegan, The Vipers, Chas McDevitt and Nancy Whiskey.

A lot of these guys still featured in coffee bars around Soho, so although the 2 I's, mainly featured Rock, there were other influences in there. These included Country, Blues, Jazz and Skiffle. It was a melting pot for musicians and their music.

So what was the 2 I's really like? Well . . . it was just a coffee bar, with room for about twenty people to stand comfortably. Behind the counter was the espresso machine and a few bottles of soft drinks. A door at the back led to the kitchen . . . but not much cooking was ever done there because it was also Tom Littlewood's office. Besides the sink and gas cooker, there was a large cupboard containing nothing but a desk diary, and on the wall there was a four-pennies-in-the-slot telephone. And that was it.

In addition to music fans the usual clientele of the 2 I's were general Soho flotsam and jetsam. Rock 'n' roll hopefuls, and other doubtfully employed characters including someone known as Jerry the Bat, a diminutive bass player and a nameless drummer straight out of Belsen. Tom Football Head, who could sing about three rock numbers, and had a job opening the curtains in a strip club was also there.

From the main coffee bar area you went down some narrow stairs to a dismal, dark and gloomy basement about the size of a large bedroom, lit by a couple of weak bulbs. At one end were a few milk crates with planks on top of them, which everybody assumed was the stage. And there may have been some sort of microphone system, left over from the Boer War. The nearest toilets were probably Piccadilly Circus Station. Later on, the walls of the 2 I's were decorated with a few photos of musicians who'd once played there, but had since moved on and now avoided the place.

Coffee bars were to the 1950s what wine bars and gastro pubs are today. To start with alcohol was not so much a part of teenage culture as it is today and, anyway, teenagers did not have the money. Coffee bars were the place to 'hang out', to use modern jargon. There were other bars in Soho, but the leading venue for us – where you could listen to skiffle and early rock 'n' roll – was undoubtedly the 2 I's. It was an exciting place for a teenager, despite being very small and rather dingy.

In those days there was no air-conditioning of any kind in such small establishments. The only access to fresh air was a small fan in the corner of the cellar. Everybody was sweating and smoking in those days. It was really a very unhealthy situation. But everybody loved the place.

Although I did not discover the 2 I's until early 1960, it had opened a few years earlier.

My own introduction to Soho and the 2 I's came when I was 18 or so. I left home in Clacton-on-Sea and joined the bed-sit crowd in London.

I was working at the Queen's Theatre, which corners Wardour Street and Shaftesbury Avenue. Anthony Newley was starring in 'Stop the World – I want to get off'. Also in the production were Anna Quayle, the Baker Twins and Marti Webb. It was great show, I remember. Some nights, after the evening performance at the Queen's finished, some of us used to walk just round the corner to Old Compton Street and go to the 2 I's.

The actual premises were really quite small, possibly no more than 5 metres wide at ground level and maybe 9 metres long with another 2 metres at the back. In 1956 many people squeezed into the almost claustrophobic space to watch artists at the birth of their careers. These included Cliff Richard, Tommy Steele, Adam Faith and Chas McDevitt.

The Irani brothers – originally there were three of them – who owned the building – used the first letter of their name for the venue. They also had interests in The Tropicana, later to be known as The Establishment Club.

But it really started to become known from April 1956 when the lease was taken over by Ray Hunter and Paul Lincoln, both Australian wrestlers. Paul had actually arrived in Britain in 1951 with only about £20 in his pocket. Along with Ray Hunter he started to look for a way to make a good life.

Their publicity and marketing skills really put the place on the map. By March 1957 it had become the premier coffee bar and attracted visitors from all over the country. Paul was instrumental in promoting some of the big early pop music shows in the country. He managed artists such as Terry Dene, The Most Brothers and Lance Fortune.

Although the 2 I's was in some ways dominant it was not the only bar of note in the mid-to-late-1950s.

At that time another coffee bar opened up. 'The Heaven and Hell' was owned by Eric Lindsay and Ray Jackson. 'Heaven' was brightly lit on the ground floor and 'Hell' was the dark basement. So successful was the club that business dropped through the floor at the 2 I's and it was under threat of closure.

Then along with the Soho Fair Wally Whyton appeared and went into the 2 I's. The Soho Fair was organized by the Soho Association and coincided with Bastille day. It was designed to bring together all the various nationalities who lived in the community. That was the turning point.

Many years ago Wally recalled,

'We went inside for a coffee and asked Paul if we could do a bit of busking. I realized he'd only been open about three weeks and was doing no trade whatever. He agreed and we went down to the basement. We started playing and it seemed that within minutes the place was busy. It seemed to work well and Paul asked us to make a regular stop over. Within a short time the place was jumping'.

Within a matter of months the 2 I's became a haven for budding managers and agents on the look out for new talent.

Later, in 1956 a young man called Lionel Bart, who co-wrote 'Rock With a Caveman' – a hit for Tommy Steele – decided that the 2 I's needed sprucing up. A lover of colour, he considered the place was a bit drab so set about painting the walls.

Unfortunately, as it was later noted, he had not mixed the paint properly and so when someone leaned on the walls their clothes often got stained with paint.

When Lionel Bart was six years old a teacher told his parents that he was a musical genius. His parents gave him an old violin, but he did not apply himself and the lessons stopped. At the age of sixteen he obtained a scholarship to St. Martin's School of Art but he was expelled for 'mischievousness'. He never learned to read or write musical notation but this did not stop him from becoming a highly significant personality in the development of British rock and pop music.

The 2 I's Coffee Bar, which has come to be known as the birth place of British rock 'n' roll, was commemorated on Monday 18th September

2006 with the award, by Westminster City Council, of a green plaque. The event was organized by Bob Mandry. The plaque reads:

'Site Of The 2 I's Coffee Bar (1956–1970) Birthplace Of British rock 'n' roll And The Popular Music Industry. Around the edge is 'City Of Westminster' and 'Robert Mandry'.

Brian Bennett attended the ceremony together with Cliff Richard, Big Jim Sullivan, Brian Locking, Tony Belcher, Clem Cattini, Dudley Fuller, Barney Smith, Wee Willie Harris, Chas McDevitt, Bruce Welch, Rick Hardy, Neil Christian, Russ Sainty, Paul Lincoln, Bobby Woodman, Tex Makins, Vince Eager, John Pilgrim, Johnny D'Avensac, Micky Green, Howard Tibble, Dave Travis, Roger La Verne, Danny Rivers, Buddy Britten, Ken Cook, Tony Annis, Michael Fogerty and John Allison. Sue Meehan, Mary Whyton, Iris Little and Peri Lewis (widow of Vince Taylor) were also present.

The Boulevard owner Ian Shaw happily gave permission for the plaque to be sited.

Stop the Music

'Right in the middle of this he would shout "stop the music"'
Ron Gould

Ron Gould of The Southern Skiffle Group remembers Iron foot Jack and other characters.

'I remember him – as a great character. He actually had an iron foot and always dressed in a large hat, tailcoat, cravat with wing collar and carried a walking stick. He would con anybody out of anything. He had an associate called Martin Windsor who later worked with Redd Sullivan, I remember.

Soho was in fact a little village in those days, and almost everybody knew everybody else. I do remember there were two basic rules. You never asked anyone where they had been and you never asked them what they did for a living.

I remember I used to bump into people like Jack Spot and Albert Dimes. I can recall the day I saw Spot throw Dimes through a greengrocer's window.'

Indeed Ron knew most of the characters in the area as his father ran a pub called The Ship which was on the corner of New Cavendish Street – on the edge of Soho.

Ron was away at boarding school until 1955 but when he came home for the school holidays he always wandered around the area quite happily homing in on the live music venues.

'The first time I ever saw any live music – skiffle – was in the Breadbasket. Wally Whyton was playing there. Then when I left school I got a job in Ralph Davis' Radio shop, which was in Brewer Street. Then I really got to know some of the local characters.

Some days when I left work – about 5.30 p.m. I suppose – I just wandered around. There was music beginning everywhere.

I think the first person I ever saw singing at the I's was Elton Hayes who sang with a small guitar. At first the bar was just that – a coffee bar. Then Hayes appeared from nowhere and started to sing. Fairly soon there was all kinds of stuff going on down there.

Traditional jazz, skiffle and so forth.

Next door to the 2 I's I recall was a deli run by Johnny Orlando, who was known as "Johnny the Pole". It was a proper deli with fridges and cold meats and salami hanging in the window. In the evening he would clear all the deli stuff from the window, turn off the fridges and cover them with blankets so people could sit on them.

Various skiffle bands used to play there. Right in the middle of this he would shout "Stop the music". He'd then jump up onto the fridge and recite "The Bespoke Overcoat" by Wolf Mankowitz (the original story was written by Nikolai Gogol). This became such a ritual that after a while some people in the audience would automatically shout 'Johnny do "The Coat".'

Ron was playing at the 2 I's with the Southern Skifflers.

'There were four of us – with me on the bass and John Pilgrim on washboard. We also used to go busking and in a couple of hours often picked up around £20, a fortune in 1956. We regularly had big crowds around us, so much so that the police had to move them on because they were blocking half the road.

A particularly good busking spot was a bomb site – right next door to the Admiral Duncan pub, sadly bombed in more recent times. The ground had been flattened and cleared and it was full of budding musicians busking their hearts out.

But it's funny looking back on it. I remember one day I was in my dad's pub when John Pilgrim came round. We were going out to do music. I had my T-chest bass and John had his washboard. My dad said, "How can you play on a scrubbing board?".

Later I showed my dad a record of the Ken Colyer Skiffle group – a 78 rpm record. On the back was the line-up including Bill Colyer on washboard. My dad said, "Yeah, but that's a real musical one".

One particular guy I knew was Mike Pratt back in the old Skiffle, Jazz and Blues days, when we lived in houses in Baylis Road and Pearman Street, Lambeth. The Baylis Road house where Pratt lived was called The Yellow Door. You can guess why.

One night we were out busking and were stopped by the police who took all our names. Mike said that his name was John Henry and that his job was Steel Driver. Old Jazz and Blues fans will get the joke.

We all corpsed but the copper had no idea what it was that was funny. My last meeting with Mike was in The Dumpling Inn on Gerrard Street. He'd just got back from India, and we had a great meal and reminisce. Never saw him again, but he was a great mate and I still recall him to mind regularly.'

Mike Pratt was, in fact, an accomplished jazz musician, playing piano and guitar, and in 1956, Lionel Bart introduced him to another friend at a party – a young sailor named Tommy Hicks.

They formed a group called The Cavemen, named after The Cave, the coffee bar under the arches near the Embankment where they used to play. They began playing in pubs and coffee bars for ten shillings a night.

Ron mentioned Elton Hayes who was well known to radio and television audiences of the 1950s as 'the man with the small guitar'. After making his radio debut on *Children's Hour*, Hayes occupied the guest star slot on every major radio variety programme of the period. He occasionally presented *Housewives' Choice*, and on *Children's Hour* he sang Edward Lear's nonsense rhymes. His version of 'The Owl and the Pussy Cat' was recorded by Parlophone and became a regular item on *Children's Favourites*.

Golden Rule in Soho

'The golden rule in Soho was not to ask questions'
Bob Jackson

Albert Dimes was known to many people including Bob Jackson who kindly sent me his recollections of the 2 I's and the area. Bob worked in Soho for over fourteen years.

'It was mid 1958 when I started work at 20 Greek Street in what today we would call a DIY store.

The premises was a Grade II listed building, with a wrought iron swivel-gib crane fixed to part of the façade. It was used in the days before "off-the-shelf" paints, when large barrels of white lead powder, turpentine and a range of pigments were offloaded from horse-drawn carts and lowered into the cellar.

We used to mix paints for artists as well as the Saint Martins School of Art and Slade School of Fine Art.

One of our customers was Francis Bacon, and I had to deliver to his studio in Kensington, which was a former stable.

I remember I arrived at mid-morning, but got no response from knocking on the door. A passing neighbour helped me by picking up a handful of gravel from the driveway and throwing it at the upstairs window. After a few minutes a very groggy looking Mr. Bacon shuffled down the stairs from his hayloft bedroom to let me in.

The scene inside was one of utter devastation. A sink and draining board were covered by unwashed mugs, plates and discarded milk cartons all mixed up with tubes of oil colour, old paint rags and brushes. The place was cluttered with canvas, frames and stretchers and an interior door was daubed with patches of paint where he had tried out various colours.

I declined his offer of a mug of tea.

My working day was usually interesting with perhaps a phone call from Basil Hume who was then head of Ampleforth College in Yorkshire and would ring up for supplies.

Mid morning I would pop over to the French Boulangerie and make polite conversation with Lord Mountbatten who was often in the queue.

Lord Mountbatten was taking a break from filming his *Life and Times* TV series at the De Lane Lea studio which was next door to our shop. He would often wander along Greek Street munching his croissants while looking in the various windows – there was not a security man in sight, unless his driver was just that.

His Jaguar was a two-tone blue but, instead of the usual mascot, there was a model of a sailor with two signal flags. The driver told me it was "something rather salty."

I sometimes used to spend my coffee breaks in the 2 I's as well as enjoying many evenings there rocking to the music from the basement.

The most frequent appearances were made by The Shadows, but also such oddball characters as Wee Willie Harris and Erky Grant. I recall Harris with his close cropped, coloured hair.

Down in the basement where the musicians performed, the music was so loud with the amplification that it may have sounded strange, but I preferred to listen from the ground floor coffee bar. The basement though was the place to experience the true atmosphere, with The Shadows being my particular favourites.

I recall Tony Meehan's drum kit being mounted on a couple of pallet boards, which had hardboard sheets tacked on top. The sheets came from my place of work which Paul Lincoln and Ray Hunter collected and carted away.

I remember having coffee with Hank Marvin when he and his group were off duty.

I missed seeing Tommy Steele at the coffee bar, but years later, he parked his Jaguar outside our premises and came in to buy some decorating materials.

The golden rule of Soho in those days was never ask questions and it was with that in mind that I had frequent conversations over coffee with Albert Dimes.

On one occasion we were sitting outside a café when two men walked past. Albert excused himself and got up to speak to them. He then brought me over and introduced them to me. Their names were Ronnie and Reggie (Kray) from the East End.

On another occasion I was having lunch in the Capitol Chinese Restaurant in Old Compton Street, seated alone at a table for four, when in walked Christine Keeler and Mandy Rice-Davis, who asked if they could join me. They were taking a break from the Profumo court case.

Mandy was the more attractive of the two. She was 19 years old and had pert blonde looks. It was very difficult to concentrate on my lunch.

There is a famous photo of Christine on a chair totally naked. That picture was taken on the first floor of our building by Lewis Morley in his studio there.

I got to meet two "Miss Worlds" on one day, one of whom was a customer, Jenny McAdam. She was a "hostess" at The Miranda night club in Greek Street, who had come in to order stuff for the club.

The other was an attractive dark-haired young lady who asked for her cousin, Glenn, who worked with me. When she left he told me she had been Miss Gibraltar.

We had a series of traumatic encounters with Judy Garland. She came in one day with her daughter Liza and the theatre painter from the London Hippodrome.

The plan was to have her dressing room painted to a theme of her choice and have it repeated in a cottage in Chelsea she was renting for her visit. She took all day to make up her mind, and off they went with the stock.

A couple of days later the painter came back to say that the job was finished, but when Judy went in to see it she went into full tantrum mode. She went ballistic and tore all the paper off the wall saying it was not what she had chosen. A further selection was made and they departed.

The screaming session apparently occurred three more times and I will never forget the wild haunted look in her eyes as she raved and ranted. Two days later came the news that she had been found dead in the bedroom of her rented Chelsea cottage. Very sad.'

Erky Grant and the Earwigs were a very mysterious group signed to Pye Records in 1963.

Nothing is known about the band or its members, except that they had a prematurely rough, punkish sound, especially in their recording of 'I'm A Hog For You'.

That Terrified Me

'There was something about his eyes that terrified me'
Pip Granger

The author Pip Granger whose novels include *Not All Tarts are Apple*, which won the Harry Bowling Prize for fiction, was a resident in Soho in the late 1950s. In fact she lived in a flat at 61 Old Compton Street, right next door to the coffee bar.

Being a resident in Soho she has great memories of some of the local characters.

'In the flat below us I remember lived the jazz singer Annie Ross and the drummer Tony Crombie. Our flat was on the top floor and I remember one day literally bumping into Billie Holiday on the stairs as I was running down. I apologised and she said in her deep south accent, "Okay, that's all right honey". She was very unsteady on her feet which I could not understand because she did not reek of booze, which most people around there did.

My father was one of them – he was a real Soho Boho (Bohemian), he was a wannabe writer and a pornographer. He had his porn shop above the deli, Parmigianies. On the wall outside was a huge harlequin statue.

When the I's started up I was a bit on the young side, so did not really appreciate the young men with attitude and quiffs in their hair . . . I was more interested in horses. Oh, what did I miss out on. But there were quite a number of horses in the area. All the produce that came from Covent Garden usually arrived in horse-drawn carts. Certainly the milk was delivered by a horse-drawn float.

Because my dad was on the edge of the underworld I saw some really odd characters and remember quite a lot about what went on. On one occasion Albert Dimes was in a fight with Jack Spot and they both fell

23

into the greengrocer's shop run by Hymie and his wife Sophia. I forget their surname. Anyway, Sophia was furious and hit the pair of them with the weights from the potato scales and shouted at them to get out.

Hymie was a great friend of the family and a lovely man. When I was a bit older I used to visit him regularly and he always gave me some exotic fruit, strawberries at Christmas for instance. One day I said to him that I was not coming any more because he shouldn't be giving me all this stuff ... He replied, "Never mind, I put it on the ABC (television) bill."

The only guy who really scared me was "Mad" Frankie Fraser. He frightened me, he really did. There was something about his eyes that terrified me.

One of my dad's henchmen was known as Legionnaire Jim. The story goes that he had killed a man in England and fled to join the French Foreign Legion. Apparently, even they kicked him out because he was too vicious, so he came back to Soho. I remember he was really nice and used to read me stories.

Then of course there was Fred Potter who had been a policeman in Lavender Hill, but when I knew him he was a bookies' runner. He always talked in a rhyming slang known as Polari.

One day we were walking with my dad and he suddenly said, "Pipe the widow ginger."

At that time I did not understand it, but what it means is:

pipe – look at

widow or widow Twankey – yankee

ginger or ginger beer – queer.

So, "Look at that queer yankee."

Quite clever really, and I remember Fred with great affection.

The language thing has always interested me. I remember Polari was used a lot – it comes from the eighteenth century and was used by the travelling players – and it's now coming back.

Then there was Rosie, a gay man who used to hang around Berwick Street. He always wore roses behind each ear. Sometimes known as Phyliss, he was a terrible boozer.

One of the best known characters was Iron Foot Jack who used to run scams. He would put an advert up somewhere, "How to make a fortune – send five shillings to –". If questioned, his reply would be, "Do as I have done."

His best scan though was the fish and chip con.

On one occasion he rented a virtually derelict restaurant in Dean Street. It had no electricity so he lit it with candles. He got the original menu and scrubbed out everything because we still had rationing. He then wrote the French for "fish and chips". He would take the order, shout it through to the kitchen, then a runner would race up the street to buy a portion. He then served it at twice the price.

What I do remember about the area was that it was perfectly safe for kids in those days. There was a black guy called Prince Monolulu who used to hang around in Soho square. All the locals used to leave their kids with him – I was one of them. He was totally safe and a lovely man. Ah! Happy days.'

Pip spoke of Polari, which is a complex mixture of Italian or Mediterranean Lingua Franca, Romany, backslang, rhyming slang, sailor slang, and thieves' cant. Later it expanded to contain words from the Yiddish language from the Jewish subculture which settled in the East End of London. It was a constantly developing form of language, with a small core lexicon of about twenty words including bona, ajax, eek, cod, naff, lattie, nanti, omi, palone, riah, zhoosh, TBH, trade, vada. It was revived in the 1950s and 1960s by its use by camp characters Julian and Sandy in the popular BBC radio show *Round the Horne*.

Ras Prince Monolulu, whose real name was Peter Carl McKay, was something of an institution on the British horse-racing scene from the 1920s until the time of his death in 1965. He was particularly noticeable for his brightly coloured clothing. As a tipster, one of his best known phrases was the cry 'I gotta horse!', which was subsequently to become the title of his memoirs.

He frequently featured in newsreel broadcasts, and as a consequence was probably the most well-known black man in Britain of the time. Although claiming to be a chief of the Falasha tribe of Abyssinia, the reality is that he came from the Caribbean island of St. Croix, now part of the US Virgin Islands. He styled himself as a prince after being press-ganged on one occasion, assuming that a prince would be far less likely to be shanghaied.

Other titles by Pip include *Trouble in Paradise*, *The Widow Ginger*, and *No Peace for the Wicked*.

They Were Great Days

'*They were great days*'
Jean Heath

One of the early groups were The Vipers Skiffle Group – and very soon 'skiffle' was king.

'I went to the 2 I's with friends after work,' remembers Jean Heath, a regular visitor, 'We just wandered around the area in Soho and never felt unsafe.

I remember The Vipers and also Tommy Steele playing there. I think they appeared on *Six-Five Special*. I know we couldn't get in when they were filming.

I also remember the coffee bar upstairs and the frothy stuff they sold, which was new in those days – then we all crammed down into the cellar for the music. They were great days.'

Around the mid-fifties, the year before the Soho Fair, Tommy Steele, the Bermondsey boy, came on the scene. Since childhood he had enjoyed singing to an audience and was arguably the first big name to emerge and made a big impression.

Another regular visitor to the 2 I's who remembers this era was Dorothy Hardy.

'Two friends and myself lived in a bed-sit in Earl's Court in the late fifties. We used to walk to the 2 I's. It was a lovely place, very friendly and we went downstairs to listen to music. Some evenings budding musicians would be strumming guitars. It was very relaxed. I remember Tommy used to talk to me and we became friends. He told me he would soon join the navy but hoped he would have a career in music.'

Jean mentioned The Vipers – who were arguably the first skiffle group to really hit the spot. They were one of the groups seen playing at the Soho fair in 1956 following which they took up residency at the 2 I's.

This is where the group really got going and started to pull the public in.

During their time there they certainly brought the coffee bar to the attention of the media, and the rest is history. Following their time there they toured the Moss Empires' Theatres across the country and their place at the 2 I's was taken by Les Hobeaux.

The line-up for Les Hobeaux included top guitarist Les Bennetts. The group was formed in 1957 when Les was still a student. Within a few months the group or, more correctly, Bennetts' signing for the group – now a six-man skiffle band-had a contract with EMI's HMV Records label.

That Boy is Good

'That boy is good, he'll go places'.
Micky Ashman

Ron Gould talked of skiffle with considerable knowledge but there is a debate as to the first skiffle music in Britain.

Bass player Micky Ashman recalls that:

'The first skiffle recording was played by the Humphrey Lyttelton band – the record was called "Big Cat-Little Cat". I know this for a fact because I had found a recording of it in a shop in Zurich. It was by Dan Burley & His Skiffle Boys. I brought it back and Humph liked it so I reckon that's how it started.

I then got heavily involved with skiffle and, whatever Chas McDevitt says, we were the first.

Of course, I was playing bass with Humph in the early fifties and we used to play the 100 Club in Oxford Street. When we had finished we walked through Soho to the 2 I's for coffee. I had my double bass with me and the girls hanging around used to comment "My that's a big one, darlin'. Is that a present for a good girl?"

It was the first place I can remember where you could get "foreign" coffee. It was always crowded.

Soho was lovely in those days. You could walk around without a care in the world. I was in there once with an agent who was sussing out Wee Willie Harris. "That boy is good," I remember him saying – "He'll go places."

I had done about four years with Humph and then Lynn Dutton, Donegan's manager asked me if I was interested. I was certainly keen and so did not take much persuading. I joined Lonnie, as did Nick Nicholls his drummer, and we eased ourselves into what was a great band and experience.'

29

*　　　*　　　*

'Big Cat-Little Cat' can be found on the following disc: *Humphrey Lyttelton & his Band – Classic 'Live' Concerts (LA CD253)*

Dan Burley played boogie-woogie piano at local socials and clubs in the 1920s in Chicago.

After a move to New York City, he became theatrical editor of the *Amsterdam News*. He recorded with Leonard Feather and Tiny Grimes in 1945 and with Lionel Hampton in 1946. That same year, he put together Dan Burley & His Skiffle Boys, an early skiffle ensemble which included Brownie McGhee and Pops Foster among its members.

In the 1950s Burley worked for *Ebony*. He died in 1962.

Micky Ashman has continued his music career and still works today. Over time he has played with all the greatest. He has spent much of his time freelancing, often in the company of Neville Dickie. He did form a version of the Ragtime Jazz Band in 1994 to make a cassette album following the success of one of his compositions, 'Humming Bird' when it was used during ice skating championships, which were televised world-wide. It is often forgotten just how much effect the bass had on a jazz band. Micky always had plenty of work because of his solid, swinging dependability.

Neville Dickie is an English boogie-woogie and stride piano player. He has performed all over Europe and North America. He has played on hundreds of BBC Radio broadcasts and has produced scores of records including a great many jazz recordings.

The Right Money

'The word was – he would do anything for the right money.'
Ron Bowden

When Lonnie Donegan left Chris Barber he was joined by Ron Bowden on drums for the first recording of 'Rock Island Line'. That was in 1956.

Ron Bowden recalls:

'I had started playing when I was in the RAF. Myself and a friend Ben Marshall started a quartet and began playing in the Sergeant's mess. That was in the late forties. We left the RAF in 1948. I worked around a bit and then joined Chris Barber in 1953 or '54 and was with him for a few years.

In 1959 I joined Kenny Ball and stayed – on and off – until 1999.

Of course, we were in central London very often. Soho was great in those days – everything was happening – and you could walk around anywhere anytime. There was never any fear – not like today.

I remember my wife used to work in St. Martin's Lane and she would walk through to meet me really late and without a second thought. That's not to say there were not crooks about, but they seemed to pick on each other.

Having said that, on one occasion I remember we were waiting to load all our gear on to a van outside the club. Dis Dizley had a guitar worth £2000. A fortune in those days. Anyway, suddenly it was noticed the guitar had disappeared. Obviously someone walking past had just picked it up.

Incredibly, two weeks later it was seen on sale in a second-hand music shop in Denmark Street for £10 so he got it back. Amazing! Obviously the thief had no idea of its value, neither did the shop, come to think of it.

The beauty of the I's was that in a sense it was a rehearsal room.

Anybody could get up and have a go. It is a pity that kind of opportunity is no longer available. The I's drew people because there was music every night and everybody knew it.

Another place we used to meet was the Soup Kitchen in St. Martin's Lane. It was a great place to go at the end of a long evening. It was started by a guy called Terence Conran who went on to make his name with Habitat.

I remember there was guy called David Lipmanoff – he was a real character. The word was he would do anything for the right money. One story that did the rounds is that following a shooting he went to Jack Spot's flat posing as a journalist to get the inside story. He was let into the flat and did not come out until two weeks later. Apparently, Jack's minders had rumbled him. What state he was in when he came out I had no idea.

Another thing he used to get up to was announcing a party for a fee at an address in say, Kensington, or somewhere so everybody would troupe over in the evening only to find the address did not exist.'

2008 marked the fiftieth anniversary of the Kenny Ball jazz band. He began his career as sideman in bands, before forming his own traditional jazz band in 1958. The band has enjoyed the longest unbroken spell of success for bands of their generation. Their traditional, 1960s hits like Samantha and Midnight in Moscow, remain popular in Dixieland and trumpet circles today.

Denmark Street or Tin Pan Alley as it is commonly known started in the 'music' business during the latter part of the 1800s. Close to Soho and all the theatres it began to specialize in sheet music – at least initially.

It was a good business and with so many musicians around, it wasn't long before the shops on the street began selling instruments – everything from violins and guitars to pianos – and the Tin Pan Alley nickname became commonplace.

In the 1950s the number of instrument retailers expanded, and with rock 'n' roll so big, the focus shifted to guitars, basses, drum kits, amplifiers and public address systems – the tools of the new groups.

I Saw A Guy Topped

'I was looking out the window and I saw a guy topped'
Raye Du-Val

Another native of Soho is the jazz drummer Raye Du-Val who was born in what was called the Latin quarter of Soho in 1932.

He recalls that Soho was a great place to grow up – it was a village where everybody knew everybody else.

'Chas McDevitt's mum lived just along the road from us.

I began my drumming career as a Caroll Levis 'discovery' and I became professional when I was fifteen. I actually turned down an opportunity to become a professional footballer with Arsenal. I was always into Jazz – still am.

I played at various jazz venues over the years including The Paris Olympia and The London Palladium. I became a great friend of Gene Krupa and his family. They put me in the Hall of Fame, although I do not consider I am worthy of such an accolade.

In the late fifties I saw the change in the music scene and found rock 'n' roll.

Of course, when I first knew the I's it was actually called the 3 I's because of the brothers who owned the place. Initially I used to go down there on a Sunday afternoon. I got to know Tony Meehan early on and in fact taught him the drums at the beginning. Brian Locking was also a regular and we often used to walk home together.

What I liked about the 2 I's was that it was so relaxed and friendly. You could go down there in your drape suit and sit on a beer barrel and slurp your coffee – trying not to spill it. You felt good to be at I's.

Of course, the guys who were discovered there are legendary but as I remember it Cliff wasn't one on them. Initially, he played across the road at the Act 1 Scene 2 coffee bar. I do remember it was Rick Richards who gave him his debut.

When I started playing I actually worked mostly for the gangsters. I remember Jack Spot and Albert Dimes. The odd thing is, you couldn't have met nicer guys – providing you didn't mess up.

Later I moved to Berwick Street, and one night I remember I was looking out of the window and I saw a guy topped. The funny thing is, next morning when I went out, there was absolutely no trace of the incident.'

Raye is best known as drummer for Emile Ford and The Checkmates, and earned a gold disc in 1959 for 'What Do you Want to Make Those Eyes at Me For?'

The group also had hits with 'Slow Boat to China' and 'Them There Eyes'.

The Beatles played as their support group before they were famous.

Raye appeared on *Oh Boy, Six-Five Special,* and *Sunday Night at the London Palladium.*

He held the title of Triple Winner of the World's Non Stop Drumming Marathon Record Contest, verified by the Guinness Book of Records, and the National Jazz Federation. The championships are recorded in the Guinness Book of Records, 1959–69.

Jack Spot, real name Jack Comer, had joined his first gang apparently when he was around seven years old. He gained the name 'Spot' because he had a big black mole on his left cheek. Jack started out as a bookie's runner, before becoming involved in a protection racket in Petticoat Lane. As time went on he moved into the West End and established himself in Soho – basically running the underworld in that area.

Blue Flames

*'The wind when ignited was blue in colour –
hence the name Blue Flames'*
Clem Cattini

Talking about drummers brings me to Clem Cattini, whose career also took off at the 2 I's.

'I remember I used to drive my old man's car down there with my kit in the back and park right outside.

However, the starting point was the film *Rock around the Clock*. It was my seventeenth birthday – 28th August 1956. It was a real turn-on for us – we just knew we had to do it. We came out of the cinema and my mate Terry Kennedy said, "Right, we'll form a group, you play the drums and I'll sing with the guitar."

My whole career started in that one crazy moment.

We formed a band called Terry Kennedy's Rock 'n' Rollers. With Mike McDonagh and Ron Prentiss on guitar and bass we started rehearsing every evening – so much so that our girlfriends complained that we did not see them enough.

Anyway, soon after we had got together we started working in a pub on a Sunday lunchtime in Lewisham. We kept the money we collected at the door and the publican made his profit behind the bar. Anyway, Terry mentioned one day that someone called Paul Lincoln had phoned and asked us to go to the 2 I's in Soho. So off we went and basically joined in a jam session.

The I's was very important because it was the birth place of British rock 'n' roll – so many people came out of there.

One thing I remember was buying Jet Harris his first amplifier. I was in the I's one night and he looked very upset. He said he'd got a new job but could not do it unless he had an amp. So we went to Denmark Street and I bought him a big red one for £75 – a lot of money in those

35

days. Then off he went with Cliff. I think he still owes it to me.

I also remember one day Tommy Steele asking if he could sing with us. He had just finished with the boats. Then Paul Lincoln opened the New 2 I's in Gerrard Street and we became the resident band there.'

In fact the 'New 2 I's was originally called the Happening 44 in Gerrard Street. It became the Beatnik HQ in the 1950s with duffel coats, and open sandals with socks and beards. It was also known at one time as The West End Jazz Club.

Later it was called the New 2 I's, but changed back to Happening 44 again in the mid 1960s – where Fairport Convention played their early gigs.

'I must just tell this funny story.

In 1958 we were touring Scotland as Billy Fury's backing group, The Beat Boys.

The lads did something that resulted in a change of name for the band. There was Kenny Packwood, Georgie Fame, Brian Gregg and me and one cold afternoon we were sat in the group van and had nothing to do so we decided to pass the time by lighting one another's farts.

You can only imagine that scene, and the loud laughter, as each of us in turn tried to out-do the others. As it was a cold day, the wind, when ignited, was blue in colour. As a consequence, from that time onward, we started to call ourselves, "The Blue Flames". A name that Georgie Fame obviously liked a lot. He used it for his own backing group in the sixties.

I also worked with, and knew well, people like Billy Fury and Vince Eager – then of course there was Bruce and Hank.

I sometimes played with them, and on occasions they would come home with me, and my wife would make them sugar sandwiches – apparently a northern delicacy.

We were and still are good friends – rumours about us falling out are a total fallacy.'

What Clem did not tell me was that he has appeared on 45 British No. 1 hits for different artists.

In October 2000 he received a Gold Badge Award for lifetime services to the music business.

It'll All be Over

'It'll all be over in a week or two'
Joe Moretti

2 I's regular Joe Moretti is a Scotsman – so known as 'Scottie'. He moved to London in 1958 to play guitar for Vince Eager and Gene Vincent:

'Well, I first saw it in 1958. My wife Pina and I arrived in London in November 1958 on a Sunday morning. We had travelled on the overnight bus from Glasgow, Scotland, and we had with us the grand sum of eleven pounds sterling in cash, two suitcases containing our clothes, and a couple of pots and pans, knives and forks etc. to set up home.

We found a bed and breakfast place and settled in for a couple of nights. I had seen Cliff Richard and the Drifters on TV back in Glasgow, and I knew that they had been discovered in the 2 I's, as had Tommy Steele.

So on the Monday evening around 6 pm, I caught the tube to Piccadilly Circus, leaving my wife at the hotel to protect our suitcases. I walked up Shaftesbury Avenue, into Wardour Street, then first right into Old Compton Street, and into the second door on the right. That's it! Or, rather, that's where it used to be.

It was just a little café with an old battered piano in the basement in Old Compton Street. But it had a soul and a buzz. A café with linoleum floors and Formica tables at street level by day, but it was downstairs, at night, under the street, that the real action took place. It was here that the record industry, fuelled by the skiffle craze, began to explode.

Everyone expected it to be a nine-day wonder. The old-timer agents would sit around in their old-timer agent restaurants, shaking their heads, muttering "It'll all be over in a week or two".'

I Was a Bit Scared

'I was a bit scared so we made our excuses and left'
Russ Sainty

The war had mercifully ended about ten years earlier and the early 1950s saw the birth of the teddy boy fashion. Soho became an odd mixture of sleaze and sex clubs, brothels and the beginning of the drugs scene.

Of course, National Service was still part of life in those days and it is strange how many people I have spoken to who came out of the services during the late 1950s and had their mind set on a career in music.

One such budding musician was Russ Sainty.

He came out of the army in July 1957 and went to The Antelope, a pub in Leytonstone one night. He remembers it well.

'There was a group called The Buddy Monroe Five. They were essentially a skiffle band but with a bit of rock thrown in. To see them was magic, until then I'd never been that close to live music. The only thing we ever had at home was a piano which mum used to play. This was freedom.

At the time I was hooked on Elvis and Gene Vincent and others. Rock 'n' roll had only just started in England with Tommy Steele's 'Rock with the Caveman'.

Rather naïvely I went up to Buddy and asked if I could sing with the Monroe Five. He told me to come back in a week with a song. So I went into Leytonstone and bought a guitar and with that learnt my three chords to do "A White Sports Coat". I went back to the pub the following week and Buddy said "Right, on you go".

It was okay and from that night I really worked at it.

Within about six weeks I actually got Buddy's band to come and back me at The Rialto in Leytonstone.

I had asked the manager if I could sing in the interval. He thought it was a great idea; remember rock 'n' roll was just kicking off.

The first time I did it my amp broke so I doubt anybody much could hear me – the applause was probably out of sympathy. Anyway he asked me back and that's when the band came – and it really started then.

It was then that I got the name Russ. I am actually Alfred Charles Sainty but the girlfriends of the Buddy band thought that Alfred was too old-fashioned so they came up with the name Russ.

I had heard about the 2 I's and knew I just had to get there – of course my parents thought I was crazy.

Soho was all of eight miles away – a foreign place.

The place was very different then – but of course being young I was very naïve – which we all were.

For instance, when I saw the ladies standing around in doorways and places I thought they were waiting for a bus or a taxi.

My dad came with me and we drove in a van I had bought and parked opposite the bar. I went in with my guitar and remember I was hit by the wonderful aroma of coffee. I just stood there and watched people coming and going and looking at the pictures on the wall – Tommy Steele and Terry Dene.

I asked for the manager and said I wanted to sing. "Right", he said, "come downstairs." Someone put the lights on and turned on a mic, which looked more like a hand grenade stuck on top of a piece of wood.

Anyway I got up and did about three numbers. "All right, that's enough", he said – he was very abrasive – "by the way I'm Tom Littlewood. If I were you I'd sling that guitar, you're not good enough on it."

Of course, I had only been playing a few weeks. He then said he'd get someone to back me. He returned a few minutes later with Tony Sheridan and we did a couple more numbers.

Tom said, "That's fine, you can come down whenever you want."

So that was that. We shook hands and I rushed back to the van. "I'm in", I said to my dad, "I've just passed the audition." That was when dad asked what they were going to pay me. Of course I hadn't thought of that – I was just so pleased to be in.

The next night I went back and I think I was there every night from around July 1958 to spring 1959 – I don't think I missed a night.

Tony backed me most nights but if he was away it was Big Jim Sullivan, Hank Marvin or sometimes Bruce. Tony Meehan was usually on drums – I think he was only about sixteen at the time. 'Liquorice' Locking was on bass.

I came off stage one night at the I's and Lionel Bart said he liked what I did and that he wanted to have a chat. We went over the road and had a drink – I remember my cousin was with us. It was about 11 p.m.

He told me he had a great song for me and he really wanted me to do it. He asked us both to go back to his place – remember I still had a job and had to get up early – plus he had a reputation for being what we now call gay. I was a bit scared so we made our excuses and left. Several months later Cliff had a massive hit with "Livin' Doll", and that was the song that Lionel had in mind for me. Ah well, that's life.

In 1960 we got a season at Butlins – I was with the Nu-Notes – that was our first professional season. We had a great time.

My days there were very special – there were some great people there – Willie Harris of course, Chas and Freddie Lloyd of The Vipers who I remember very well – he was a really nice guy.

It's funny looking back – you knew the area had a reputation but I was never scared – not like today. Yes there were the gangs, the Richardsons and the Krays but they never interfered with ordinary folk – I certainly never saw any problems.

It's hard to express how revolutionary the place was following the dark days of the war. Young people had nothing then – we just used to go to cinemas as teenagers – that was about it.'

During that time Russ was a photographic model for John Stephen of Carnaby Street – which was great publicity for him. He was pictured in the *Evening Standard* and in several Men's clothing magazines.

Russ continued his showbiz career – broadcasting with the BBC, recording and doing all the northern clubs.

He went to South Africa in 1976 to do a club circuit in Durban and Cape Town and in the early 1980s headed for Florida to work the cruise liners.

In 1982 he came back to take over as Entertainment Manager for Warner's at Sinah Warren Hotel on Hayling Island.

He still does summer seasons.

*   *   *

Russ mentioned Tony Sheridan who is an English rock 'n' roll singer-songwriter and guitarist.

He is best known as an early collaborator of The Beatles, and one of two non-Beatles (the other being Billy Preston) to receive label performance credits on a record with the group.

John Stephen moved to London from Glasgow in 1952 at the age of eighteen, and set up his first shop called 'His Clothes' in Beak Street, Soho.

By 1965, he owned eight shops in Carnaby Street, selling clothes to mod bands such as The Small Faces, and boasting David Bowie as a designer. He is remembered as one of the main figures in creating Swinging London.

In 2005, Westminster City Council unveiled a plaque in Carnaby Street commemorating his influence on fashion.

The Lights Would Start to Flash

'He used to press a button and the lights would start to flash'
Rockin' Gerry Champion

Someone else who had been doing National Service and came out of the army in March 1957 was Gerry Champion. Known then as Gerry Marshall, he had read about the 2 I's in the press.

'Everybody knew the I's was the place to be and you had to be there if you wanted to be in the scene. I started going down there in the summer of 1957.

There was a guy I remember called Fabulous Fred. He was a compere and a warm-up artist, a really funny guy; a little podgy bloke I remember. He always used to sing, "Why is everybody always picking on me?"

I was on stage one night when this fellow came up with his guitar and asked if he could join me. It was Keith Kelly who had been with the John Barry Seven. He got up and sang a song called "Cold White and Beautiful" which, if I remember correctly, was banned by the BBC.

Apparently, he gave up show business because he hated the rat race. In fact I was in touch with him quite recently – after forty odd years.

I remember seeing Terry Dene there at the time. I went down for an audition with Paul Lincoln and Tom Littlewood. I had got a job on the buses so was burning the candle at both ends – well, you can when you are young can't you?

I met several interesting guys down there; most were really friendly but the one I did not get on with was Tony Sheridan – he was not nice – not many people liked him. Anyway, I used to do a couple of nights a week down there – just spots you know.

Paul Lincoln was a bit funny about time. If you over-ran your slot he used to press a button and the lights would start to flash in your eyes – so you had to finish.

I remember Vince Taylor appeared and asked me if I would do the warm-ups for the Playboys. That was good – I got on well with him.

At one stage I was apparently known as the Tommy Steele of Stamford Hill because I used to do some of his numbers.

I had bought a guitar in 1957 for £12, a lot of money for me then. I later shared it with Peter Green, from what became known as Fleetwood Mac. He was fifteen at the time and we used to go to his brother's flat and practise – so I can say Peter learned to play on my guitar.

Another musician who I remember was Roy Young. He was terrific on the piano doing Little Richard stuff. He went on to great things.

Then in 1966 I got working with Joe Meek. I had been writing songs and he wanted to hear some of them. I did a couple of demos which he liked. He said he needed a couple of big hits because he was having a bad time money-wise during that period. However, it was not to be. Sadly in 1967 he committed suicide, as we all know.

I eventually turned professional in 1989 and did various things with a range of groups. I also did some acting and was in a few episodes of the BBC TV series *The House of Eliott*.

Nowadays I still perform but am also a member of the Magic Mummers. We go round villages acting things based on *The Canterbury Tales*.

Recently I have started writing poetry.'

Roy Young was one of rock 'n' roll's greatest entertainers with his trademark boogie-woogie piano.

By 1961, a new generation of music had begun and Hamburg, Germany was the place to be. Roy's music had reached the European market scene by this time where he regularly played the legendary stages of Germany.

Along with Tony Sheridan, and Ringo Starr they formed The Beat Brothers at the Top Ten Club in Hamburg to become the house band.

As well as performing, Young was hired by the club to enlist the talent of The Beatles, Ray Charles, Little Richard and Chuck Berry, among others.

Peter Green is a British blues-rock guitarist and founder of the band Fleetwood Mac.

A figurehead in the British blues movement, Green inspired B.B. King to say, 'He has the sweetest tone I ever heard; he was the only one who gave me the cold sweats.'

Don't Tell Your Mother

'Don't tell your mother what kind of place you work in'
Howard Tibble

It's funny how dates click in the mind. Shakin' Stevens' drummer Howard Tibble specifically remembers 1961:

'I started playing, or I should say, learning drums when I was about fourteen and I was terrible – I don't know how I got away with it. I was in a little band called Guitars Anonymous. We found the I's because it had become a land mark following Cliff so we blagged a gig and got away with it. We ended up doing every Monday night at the I's coffee bar.

My dad used to borrow one of his firm's vans and drop us off at the club – of course you could park right outside in those days. He'd come back around 11.30 p.m. and pick us up. He arrived a bit early one night and came in for a coffee.

Apparently, there was another bloke sitting there having a cup so they got chatting and in the end he asked my dad why he was there. My dad answered that he had come to pick his boys. This guy apparently replied, "You're lucky, I wish I had one!" It was probably the first time in his life my dad had met a gay man. On the way home he said "Don't tell your mother about the sort of place you work in."

The early sixties for me was a very optimistic period – you had the feeling that you could do anything and go anywhere – become someone. The era of the sixties represented a new freedom. For one thing there was no more rationing and you could be eccentric without causing trouble.

I remember one of the guys dad had a shop in Brewer Street. He used to sell professional theatrical stuff. One night Buddy got some flash powder and filled an envelope. He brought it into the I's and put this green powder stuff in a saucer. Halfway though the evening he put a match to it. Very quickly the basement filled with green smoke. It went everywhere and up through the grill to the pavement. Tom Littlewood thought the place was on fire so called the brigade. Of course, when they arrived they were very annoyed – so was Tom.

There were some great characters hanging around at the time. One of them was a stripper named Phyllis, who was a good laugh. The street girls used to use the place as a coffee stop in their "breaks" and we got to know them over the years.

One of them was a girl called Bridget Bond – she looked as if she had come from Brazil. Anyway I sort of fell in love with her – just as you do when you are fourteen years old. One day she sat me on her lap and gave me a hug and kiss – with the result that the other girls would not talk to me for a while. Later I found out that Bridget Bond was the second only sex-change woman in England – so I'd been snogged by a bloke – at fourteen. I went from hero to absolute zero.

Anyway, several years later a couple of us had a sort of sentimental night out in the West End and we ended up in a strip club for old time's sake. We gradually worked our way to the front. The lights went down and the next women strode on to the little stage all in black leather and all the gear. Suddenly, my mate turned to me and said, "Fuck me, it's Phyllis". Unfortunately, he said it too loudly because she stopped and looked down.

"Who's that?" she said, "It's Buddy and Howard," – "Cor blimey, how are you boys?"

Then all the blokes behind us started shouting "Shut up, and get 'em off."

She shouted back "Shut up, I'm talking to my mates.'"

Howard is still busy as Shakin' Stevens drummer.

Shakin' Stevens, also known as 'Shaky', is a Platinum-selling Welsh rock 'n' roll singer and songwriter, who has the distinction of being the top-selling British male singles' artist of the 1980s.

His recording and performing career spans forty years, although it was not until 1980 that he saw commercial success in his native land. In the UK alone Stevens has charted no fewer than 34 top 40 hit singles.

A Lot of Gangsters

'There were a lot of gangsters around but they never bothered us'
Chas McDevitt

It's amazing when you consider that within little more than a year the sign outside the 2 I's included the words 'famous' and 'home of the stars' with people often queuing right round the corner.

An early rising star at the 2 I's was Chas McDevitt.

In late 1956, while recording the song 'Freight Train' – written by folk blues singer Elizabeth Cotten – for Oriole Records, studio owner Bill Varley suggested they should add a female singer.

As a result, folk singer Nancy Whiskey was invited to join the Chas McDevitt Skiffle Group. At first she was reluctant to give up her folk singing but she did and they re-recorded the song with her vocals. The record became a big hit in the UK in 1957 at the height of the skiffle boom.

Chas has good memories of the area and times:

'Our association with the 2 I's started properly in 1956. We were living in Chelsea and my washboard player used to go around the coffee bars. We got £5 per night at the I's which was stupendous in those days.

One night in the 2 I's Bill Varley and Roy Tooley were there with their recording machines. They were recording The Vipers. We heard about this and wanted some of the action so we got hold of Bill and had a recording session in a small studio on Denmark Street.

The Vipers started there in July 1956. We had been busking but it started to rain so went into the 2 I's. The Vipers already had a residency there and we got lucky, also being asked to play.

Paul had a great eye for publicity and the fact that Tommy Steele came through the door did not go unnoticed. A year or so later Adam Faith also played there, but at the time he did not make any impression.

There were many other coffee bars all over the place so it was not until the *Six-Five Special* came to the 2 I's that it became "the place".

The 2 I's stood out because of the publicity and, it's funny you know, there were a lot of gangsters around but they never bothered the I's. I guess that was because the place was run by two large professional wrestlers.

Eventually, we decided to turn pro but half my original group refused, so I got some new guys in. A guitar player from a group called The Ghouls – he was also playing with The Cotton Pickers.

Les Bennetts was there with me but he was pinched by Lonnie Donegan.

Of course, there was no amplification – in the early days at least; it was all acoustic. My group had six guitars at one time. When amplification started rock 'n' roll really came on.

I remember Tommy Steele was photographed and it was suggested he played the Stork Club. Princess Margaret happened to be there – which gave a big boost to publicity for him. I also remember the King Bothers and of course Willie Harris.'

Les Bennetts' formal entry into music took place during the summer of 1957, when he was seventeen years old and still a student at London's Polytechnic School.

He formed a six-man skiffle group which, by the end of the year, was ready to turn professional. The group – or, more correctly, Bennetts' signing for the group – was given a contract with EMI's HMV Records label.

Les was a phenomenally skilled guitarist and established as a star virtually instantaneously on the burgeoning skiffle scene. In 1959, he moved to America for a time and operated clubs in various cities, including New Orleans and New York; and returned to England in the mid 1960s. He was preparing for a comeback in conjunction with the Chas McDevitt Skiffle Group in 1995 when he died of lung cancer.

Chas is still active working with people like Steve Benbow and Jack Fallon and Chas' daughter, Kerry.

The Man who Took the Biggest Cut

'He was the man who took the biggest cut from anybody he could'
Tony Annis

Music was slowly changing and that included different styles of skiffle.

Worldwide photographer and former drummer Tony Annis recalls that:

'We were the first to change skiffle because we had drums and that gave it a different beat and emphasis.

Our little group was slowly formed by George Plummer – who was actually a plumber – so that's quite funny.

He gradually got us together, so there was Michael Fogerty, Bob Mills and an Indian called Les Vas who was a rhythm guitarist and a very good one too. He was playing in a dance band. We were a very mixed bunch including two from public school.

We started by getting little gigs around US air bases all over the place. We could not however plan anything long term because we all had National Service looming on the horizon. We had about six months of freedom left so recording companies were not really interested as we would soon be on our way.

We played at the I's in 1956–57 in the basement that was very hot, I recall – sometimes it went to a hundred degrees. We did two or three nights a week for about half a crown and a free coke each night. I remember on Fridays there was a local prostitute who used to come in the place just to listen. She would lend me enough money to get a cab home, and I would repay her on Monday. Trust was all in those days. Sadly, that kind of spirit is gone today, don't you think?

We also did the odd night at the Skiffle Cellar, but the I's was the place.

Another thing about the I's was that if you went in at lunchtimes the jukebox was full of discs of the people who played there – so they got double exposure, if you like.

I do recall the Most brothers. Mickie Most was influenced by skiffle and early rock 'n' roll in his youth and had worked as a singing waiter at the 2 I's. He had formed a singing duo with Alex Wharton to become The Most Brothers. They scored a minor hit with Decca Records called 'Takes a Whole Lotta Loving to Keep My Baby Happy' before disbanding. Mickey was always complaining about how everybody was ripping him off. Although he had a decent car and lots of suits he got very little actual money. However, later in life he was the man who took the biggest cut from anybody he could. Anyway, we became the Blue Jeans until we were called up.

We actually were voted the third best group by *Melody Maker.*

Then a bunch of lads from Liverpool tried to pinch the name. Well, it was established so it would have given them a head start. However, George Plummer was not having any of that and complained, so they added the word "Swinging".'

In November 1957 Tony went into the forces for his National Service and on returning to civvy street spent many years in the film and television industry. More recently he has become an established photographer with expeditions to many parts of the world including some remote areas of South America.

While Tony was playing at the 2 I's his young sister, Francesca, came in and sang 'Freight Train' at the age of about fourteen. She was wearing little blond pigtails, she told me, and 'pedal pushers.'

Francesca Annis trained as a ballet dancer and then studied drama at the Corona Stage Academy. Francesca began acting professionally in her teens, and made her film debut in the 1950s. In 1967 she played Estella in a television adaptation of *Great Expectations.* She also presented children's television programmes. Francesca went on to become one of our best actresses appearing in a great many television and stage productions.

He Shot Himself in the Foot

'I think later he shot himself in the foot'
Michael Fogerty

A fellow member of the Blue Jeans was the bass player Michael Fogerty who recalled what he described as some of the happiest days of his life.

'It was a hell of a lot of fun really. But the strange thing was that out of that era came, by my standards, a little clutch of people who were seriously good. That, of course, is in addition to Cliff, Tommy and Adam Faith.

There was never any anger or envy; everybody got on well and we just did our music.

Looking back, the astonishing thing is how innocent we were compared to the youth of today, and I bet we were a lot happier. We did not drink, basically because we could not afford it and to this day I have never taken drugs. We were a perfectly innocent bunch of lads, only interested in girls and skiffle.

Soho, of course, had a slightly racy reputation in those days but you have to remember we were not much over seventeen years old and still had some growing up to do. We were innocents abroad you might say.

But what I do remember about the I's was that it was a bloody death trap. Just one flight of stairs down and the place was crammed full, with most people smoking. When you think of it like that, it was a really unhealthy place to be, I suppose. But the atmosphere of the place was wonderful. Obviously, some of the bands were better than others, but at the time we were around The Vipers were king.

Having got our group together we started doing various gigs and learnt as we went along. After a while we entered a skiffle competition in what used to be the Town Hall in Kensington High Street. Amazingly we won, and I've still got the cup.

We went on to enter another competition, which was called the All Britain Skiffle Contest held in Loughton, which we also won. Chas McDevitt was the judge. I reminded him of this when we met at the unveiling of the plaque. Of course he could not remember it as he had judged a large number of similar events.

One of our band, George Plummer, who was sort of the leader went in to the 2 I's and spoke to Ray Hunter and asked if we could play there. This resulted in us being there the following night, then doing a series consisting of two sets a night. I think we earned a couple of bob each plus a free coffee, if we were lucky.

Our band used to alternate with The Vipers and Adam Faith's The Worried Men.

I remember Adam in the early days; only he was Terry then and he worked as a film cutter in Wardour Street. I can see him now sitting on the edge of the stage wearing jeans that looked as if they had been made from a butcher's apron. He was swigging from a bottle of cough mixture. Somebody actually said he was a bit of a hypochondriac. He was only a little guy but very good looking.

One night I was talking to Bob Mills who told me Terry was going to go solo and change his name. I can recall the two of us slightly sniggering because although he was a very nice guy he really did not sing very well. However within six months he had his first number one hit.

At the time I was living in Earl's Court and I remember dragging this damn great T-chest bass on the tube, and getting funny looks. I often used to run up the escalator with the T-chest, pole and string. We were never late. In fact it was Tony's mum who told us how important it was to be on time.

"If you are late somebody else will get the job." Of course, she was right.

A bit later I became a medical student at Barts – which was a huge mistake – and as a result began to miss some nights. Jet Harris stood in for me on those nights.

Jet, of course, went on to be a member of The Shadows and then I think he shot himself in the foot by going off with Tony Meehan.

But looking back at The Blue Jeans I think we could have really gone somewhere.

On one occasion a West Indian guy asked us if he could join The

Blue Jeans but we turned him down. Later we realized our mistake when Emile Ford had a huge hit with "What Do You Want to Make Those Eyes at Me For?".

I also remember Tony's sister, Francesca Annis. I guess she would have been about twelve years old and was at the Corona Stage Academy, now known as the Ravenscourt Theatre School. One day she sang "Freight Train", doing all the hand gestures. She was the youngest person ever to appear at the I's. I expect she was only allowed there because Tony was with her. I am sure he frog-marched her home afterwards.'

Michael did not follow a musical career but went into the insurance and finance business, retiring just a few years ago.

Emile Ford is a musician and singer, who was popular in the late 1950s and early 1960s.

He teamed up with George Ford, Ken Street and John Cuffley as Emile Ford and The Checkmates, and their first self-produced recording 'What Do You Want to Make Those Eyes at Me For?' went to number one in the UK Singles Chart at the end of 1959 and stayed there for six weeks.

It was winning the Soho Fair talent contest in July 1959, that led to his Pye recording contract.

Only the Bits that We Were Allowed

'Only the bits that we were allowed to hear'
Betty Osment

A regular visitor to the I's who has memories of the early days is Betty Osment. She recalls:

'Memories of the 2 I's and other coffee bars, how they abound; other coffee bars were okay, but the 2 I's was the one, the one and only. Where else could you have counted Cliff Richard, Mickie Most, Bruce Welch, Hank Marvin, to name but a few amongst friends at that time?

I was there when Tommy Steel got engaged to Ann; I noted it in my diary. I remember Bruce's wedding to his first wife; it was on Easter Saturday.

I also recall Brian Bennett asking Margaret to marry him.

The 2 I's was a small place, but it had something, an indefinable something. Maybe it was us, teenagers, the first breed. Maybe it was postwar austerity; maybe it was *Blackboard Jungle*, Elvis; but that era has never been re-created.

I am so proud to have been part of that era and treasure my memories of days filled with laughter, fun, living, loving, talking, hanging about, just being young. We all gelled. Vince Taylor was a great laugh, Jet Harris not so, more serious – moody even. Hank and Bruce great fun. Hank has a wonderful sense of humour, Tony Meehan, serious to a point. Oh, I could go on and on.

It is so sad about Rick Hardy, who was a great one for the 2 I's and did a lot to promote it; he was a lovely guy and a good singer.'

Betty remembered Brian Bennett the drummer, pianist, composer, arranger and record producer of popular music. He started playing for a skiffle group in Ramsgate when he was sixteen. After returning to London he became the in-house drummer at the 2 I's Coffee Bar in Soho and was a regular on Jack Good's TV show *Oh Boy!* Later he became a member of Marty Wilde's Wildcats, and then, in October 1961, he joined Cliff Richard and The Shadows as the replacement for Tony Meehan.

Rick Hardy became a regular performer at the 2 I's coffee bar, as Adam Faith's replacement in the Worried Men. Later he appeared with a young singer named Harry Webb, who went on to find fame and fortune as Cliff Richard. In 1960 he was playing with the Jets who became the first English rock 'n' roll band to play in Hamburg, with The Beatles following in their footsteps several weeks later. His career developed with a ten-year stint performing at American Forces bases all over the world. Eventually he returned to England and created a cockney act based on his London roots appearing in a role as the Pearly King in the film *Trainspotting*. Sadly, he was killed in a car crash towards the end of 2006.

Betty continued,

'I remember one day about September time a lovely girl came in. She was aged sixteen, called Christina – she was on a visit from South Africa "doing Europe" with her parents, and, and of course had to see the 2 I's.

Mickie Most was there and they had a chat, of course the girl came again, as she found it so wonderful; her father used to drop her off and pick her up.

She met Mickie most times, and they fell in love. Yes, corny I know, but they did, and then she returned to South Africa.

They corresponded and Mickie would bring the letters to us and read them; at least the bits that we were allowed to hear; then we would tell him what to say to Christina from us.

But true love would last out, and in December Mickie flew over to South Africa – they got married in February, and this marriage lasted until Mickie died a few years ago. She was such a lovely girl; dark haired and pretty. Mickie was smitten; she was a lot younger than him, but love conquered all.

This probably went on in lots of places, but as it turned out the 2 I's and its occupants were different; it's just that we didn't know.

I remember Tony Meehan came in one Friday to tell us he had a spot on the Saturday Show in the morning, so I said "who do you think will get up to listen to you?" We never took this fame thing seriously; what an eclectic mix we were.

A mish-mash of people made up the 2 I's. Wonderfully mad, funny, but all got on. I would go to it any time any day as there was always someone there. I would go on my own or with friends.'

Mickie Most started out as a rock 'n' roll performer, finding success with a string of hits when he went to South Africa. He made his mark in music as one of the most successful British producers of the 1960s and 1970s. He discovered, and was the first producer for The Animals and Herman's Hermits, and he also produced for Donovan and The Yardbirds.

Brian Holden, later Vince Taylor, aged eighteen, was impressed by the music of Gene Vincent and Elvis Presley. He began to sing, mostly at amateur gigs at the beginning. Joe Barbera, his brother-in-law, became his manager.

When Joe went to London on business he asked Vince to join him to check out the music scene. In London, Vince went to the 2 I's where Tommy Steele was playing.

There he met drummer Tony Meehan and bass player Tex Makins. They formed a band called The Playboys.

Whilst looking at a packet of Pall Mall cigarettes he noticed the phrase, 'In hoc Vince's', thus giving rise to his new stage name of Vince Taylor.

During 1961 and 1962, Vince toured Europe including The French Riviera, Brussels, Belgium, Spain, and The Netherlands, with Bobbie Clarke's band, once again called Vince Taylor and the Playboys (in French this was translated as 'Vince Taylor et ses Play-Boys'. However, although dynamic on stage, his unpredictable personality caused several arguments within the band, and The Playboys fired Vince Taylor and changed their name to 'The Bobbie Clarke Noise'.

This all happened just before a major concert in Paris.

Despite his sacking Taylor remained friendly with the band and they asked if he could come to Paris too.

He gave an amazing performance at the sound check that the organizers decided to put Vince at the top of the bill. As a result of his performance at those two shows, Eddie Barclay signed him to a six-year record deal on the Barclay label.

Vince Taylor, in fact, reputedly ran the Top Ten Club in D'Arby Street during the later part of the 1950s.

Bobby Clarke was the first drummer in Europe, and quite possibly the first rock drummer in the world to use a double bass drum kit with special pedals, long before Ginger Baker or Keith Moon.

No One Discovered Us

'And absolutely no one discovered us'
Sir Cliff Richard

Nobody knew at that time what big names they would become. The 2 I's was just a great atmosphere where musicians turned up to play – often for little or no money.

One who attended and spoke at the plaque ceremony was Sir Cliff Richard.

Cliff shared some memories with me.

'Elvis was king though he hadn't been crowned! And Tommy Steele was being hailed as the UK's answer to him.

I wanted to be "Elvis" with the quiff hair – everything. Obviously, I used to use Brylcream but tried other stuff as well. On one occasion I even used lard but it just stank.

Me and my friends were still in school but about to leave. Of course, we knew that Tommy and, quickly on his heels, Terry Dene, had been discovered at the 2 I's and we were desperate to get there to compete.

So one night we just showed up and said we'd like to play, and they said, "Okay, come back next week." It was as easy as that! We played every night from Monday to Friday – and absolutely no one discovered us!

But two things did happen. A guy who ran a ballroom offered us a job one night only and, because he wanted a name to front The Drifters, "Cliff Richard" was born.

The second thing was meeting Jan Vane, who thought we were so good she wanted to start a fan club – what excellent taste she had! – and her club eventually became the biggest in Britain.

But the experience at the 2 I's was awesome for us as young musicians

– having a nightly audience that was excited by what we were doing was fantastic. I'll never forget that sweaty little "cave" in Old Compton Street and us with our new shirts bought specially for the occasion. At one end there was a stage, but there was no backstage as such, so we fought our way down, played, and then fought our way back to get a juice or coffee before heading home.

I don't think that amateurs are allowed to drop in and play at clubs these days. What a loss of opportunity for the clubs and the amateurs.

For me, the 2 I's played a vital part in my career. I played to my first rock audience and, though I wasn't "discovered" there, I did discover myself. I knew what I wanted to be, and had the feeling that I could make it!

The 2 I's is forever part of British rock history, as is The Cavern in Liverpool, but the 2 I's led the way by a good few years and played a major role in many music careers. Had I never been there of course, I would never have found Hank, Bruce or Tony Meehan. For that alone, the 2 I's has my eternal thanks!'

Jan Vane, was taken to the 2 I's one Saturday night by her boyfriend as a treat for her sixteenth birthday. Never having been anywhere like the 2 I's before, she had the impression that if Cliff was playing there he must be famous. She stayed behind after the show and asked Cliff if he had a fan club. Cliff said no but liked the idea so she became fan club secretary.

Bruce Welch of The Shadows, who was at the plaque ceremony, had found the 2 I's in April 1958. As he has said it was a place for what today we call wannabees.

Everybody knew about it because Tommy Steele had supposedly been discovered there in 1956.

He had teamed up with Hank Marvin and had worked four nights a week for about five months – for the equivalent of 80p per night for a four-hour set.

During his time there he met Jet Harris and Tony Meehan. On the nights he wasn't singing he would go downstairs and try and sell orange juice.

One night he said a guy came down – Cliff and the Drifters. He had real charisma, according to Bruce. Today, most people seem to be on a charisma by-pass.

By September 1958 Hank was very well known at the 2 I's along with Tony Sheridan – they were a great team.

Apparently, one afternoon Cliff's manager, John Foster, came down and offered Hank the chance to join Cliff's band. Hank said 'Only if my mate Bruce can come as well.'

So, they went off to a tailor's shop in Dean Street where Cliff was being fitted with some stage gear. They all boarded a Green Line bus to Cliff's family home in Cheshunt where they auditioned. They did about twenty minutes and Cliff said, 'Right, you're in.'

It Was a Right Dump

'When I first went there I thought it was a right dump'
Big Jim Sullivan

Cliff spoke of the facility for amateur musicians to have a place where they could try out their ideas, which sadly doesn't exist anymore.

Trying out meant you probably needed to own a musical instrument – rather than always borrowing one.

One of the great guitarists that came out of that time and place was Big Jim Sullivan. He remembers his first instrument.

'As a lad I was living with my grandparents and used to go over to my sister's place near Notting Hill Gate once a month. She had an old guitar that stood in the corner of her living room – so one day I just picked it up and simply fell into it. It seemed to come naturally.

I remember I played "Zambezi" which was popular at the time. Anyway, I went home and asked if I could have a guitar. Well, there wasn't much money around so the answer was probably not. In the meantime my sister had pawned it for a £1. So I had to get hold of that much to get it back from the shop.

I had it for a couple of weeks, then my dad came over and I asked him to help me get a better one. He thought about it then said he would and I suppose I never looked back. Later on, I got hold of a 'Black Row', which I kept for a couple of years.

In about 1954–55 I was in a band called the Clay County Boys. We were a country band and we used to tour the American bases over here. It was great and I really learned a lot.

I was down at the 2 I's, I suppose, from 1956 or 57.

Before that I used to go down the Skiffle Cellar – that's before skiffle was really popular. It was in its very early stages with people like Rambling Jack Elliott, Sonny Terry and Brownie McGhee.

63

When I first went down to the I's I thought it was a right dump. But it drew people because it was the only rock 'n' roll place in town. There were other popular venues – The Flamingo Club and Ronnie Scott's for instance – but they were very jazz orientated.

We would go down the I's and just have a jam session whenever we liked – usually for no money. When we did get any it was Tom Littlewood who paid out. I remember he used to stand at the top of the stairs with a thick bunch of fivers in his hand. It looked a fortune in those days.

One night, Tex Makins and Bobby Woodman came and asked me to play for Marty Wilde. They said he had heard me play and wanted me to join his band – on one condition – I had to dye my hair blonde. So, like a fool I had it done and became a "Wildcat". I guess that was around late 1957.

Other guys who were involved in that were Brian "Liquorice" Locking and Brian Bennett.

There were a couple of others but after a few weeks Marty sacked them because in his opinion they did not have the finesse that he expected.

Through Marty I met Jack Good who used me in all his studio recordings.

"Liquorice" and Brian were part of the resident rhythm section at the I's at one time – and actually got regular money.

So the years flew by and in 1978 I joined James Last and was with him for ten years. It was then that I began to wind down a bit.

I enjoyed every bit of it – I never wanted to be a "star", but always a back up man.'

In more recent times Jim and guitarist Doug Pruden toured as the BJS Duo. Doug also played in the Big Jim Sullivan Band with Duncan McKenzie, Malcolm Mortimer and Pete Shaw.

In 2006 Sullivan was featured in the 'Guitar Maestro' DVD series.

Jim is still at it and a few days after we chatted he was off to the continent to run some master classes. It seems nearly all the musicians I have had the privilege of meeting have no intention of actually retiring. As they say 'If you enjoy something, why stop doing it?'

Well, you cannot argue with that.

Bobby Woodman played on the Vince Taylor classic 'Brand New Cadillac', and his reputation as a class drummer soared.

By 1961 he had moved on and was still using his real name Bobby Woodman, with his own band The Bobby Woodman Noise, the band played the prestigious Olympia in Paris, with Wee Willie Harris down to top the bill.

Vince Taylor came along as a friend of the band, as he had never been to France. His sound-check astounded the back-stage crew and his billing was changed to topping the show. He was immediately offered a deal and Vince and the Playboys signed to the Barclay label for a six-year deal.

Quite a Clown

'He was always smiling – quite a clown'
Lynn Terry

Another admirer of Brian 'Liquorice' Locking was Lynn Terry. Like me Lynn, who I mentioned earlier in the book, was a regular visitor who just loved the place and the people. She recalled the first time she went there:

'Actually my first visit to the 2 I's was in 1958. It was known as the mince pies or the mincers.

There was a resident group. Vince Taylor was there and I remember in 1959 Brian "Liquorice" Locking and Brian Bennett played in a group called The Playboys.

"Liquorice" was a great bloke – always smiling and quite a clown. One of the numbers they did was "Charlie Brown". He always sang the line "Why is everybody always picking on me?" He really emphasized that line. I also remember when Tom Littlewood promoted Lance Fortune and Keith Kelly. He gave me some cash to buy their records from a stall in East Ham market to help boost record sales. Probably others did as well.

I was there the first time Dave Berry sang and he was the only singer I heard to get a really sustained applause at that time.

Later, I met "Liquorice" in Coventry when I was visiting family in 1970. We went to a pub called the White Horse. "Liquorice" recognized me and wanted to say hello but my husband was very possessive and I wasn't able to talk to him.

The 2 I's was a great place to be. It was friendly, intimate and boy, did it rock. The youngsters today would probably think it was quite tame but there was no binge drinking, no fights, just the greatest music ever.'

Lance Fortune, whose real name was Chris Morris, had begun life in a group formed in Birkenhead School – The Firecrests.

His No. 4 chart hit "Be Mine" was produced by Joe Meek and was the first hit Meek had as a solo producer. Fortune also hit the charts with "This Love I Have For You". He later left the Parnes stable and gave up singing for a while to run a club in Portsmouth.

Later in the sixties he was then invited to join a vocal group, The Staggerlees.

It's interesting to note that when Lance left him, Parnes gave the name Lance Fortune to a new signing, Clive Powell from Leigh, Lancashire. There were now two Lance Fortunes, until Clive suggested he have another name and became Georgie Fame.

Larry Parnes was the first major British rock manager, and was easily the most successful in the early rock era. Establishing a pattern that he was to follow consistently, Parnes renamed Tommy Hicks, Tommy Steele and Reg Smith, who was given the name Marty Wilde. Others included Georgie Fame, Lance Fortune, Duffy Power, Johnny Gentle, Vince Eager and Dickie Pride. The only member of the stable to resist Parnes' renaming process was the Lincolnshire-born Cockney Joe Brown – Larry wanted him to become Elmer Twitch.

On the music front various other venues were coming to life.

In the early to mid 1950s Alexis Korner and Cyril Davies were running weekly blues sessions at the Roundhouse pub in Wardour Street on the corner of Brewer Street. Others who played there included Rory McEwan.

The Princess Louise pub, which was situated in Holborn used to stage what was known as 'hootenanny' a sort of American folk music, perhaps not unlike ceilidh.

Skiffle and the coffee bars were beginning to open up and for a while in 1956 almost every Soho door and window seemed to produce music of one sort or another.

Another influential Skiffle and folk venue was undoubtedly the Bread Basket. This was very much 'in' with many musicians, the then owner being a big fan.

Coffee was served in glass mugs or cups which now and again used to 'explode'.

Ron Gould tried to enlighten me about this bizarre happening . . .

'A professor explained that the type of glass they were made of did not reverberate so it stored up the energy from whenever they were knocked – then suddenly they would shatter if they were put down a little hard. You can imagine the reaction – just think – you put a coffee cup down and it disintegrates with coffee all over the place.'

He Wanted 60 Percent

'He wanted 60 percent of our earnings – outrageous'
Danny Rivers

It's funny how today we think of young teenagers and their connection with society. 'There's nothing to do' we hear all too often. Well, it was just the same back then, only with a lot less money. But we just got on with it and made our own entertainment. We used our imagination, which had not been withered away by television or computer games.

Or we had an objective and went for it, as Danny Rivers did.

As a fifteen-year-old in 1957, Danny Rivers remembers the 2 I's as very crowded so he only went a few times.

'I do recall Vince Taylor and of course Wee Willie Harris, but it was about 1960 when I really started seeing acts. I worked with Chas Hodges and Billy Grey and The Stormers and it really took off towards the end of 1960.

We entered a talent competition at the Finsbury Park Ballroom – we did one number and got a contract to work at Filey holiday camp.

Larry Parnes and Joe Meek saw us and we were "in". I did three records for Joe – he always liked what we did. The trouble with Larry was that he wanted 60 per cent of our earnings, which was outrageous and my dad would not agree. I've actually still got the contract.

I was making records for Top Rank with Dick Rowe.

I actually stopped in mid 1960s and it was not until the early 1990s that I got going again. Life goes in circles.'

Danny has appeared at several recent gigs in association with *Tales from the Woods* and 2 I's gatherings.

Dick Rowe was, in fact, one of the most important producers of middle-of-the-road hits in the 1950s and early 1960s, along with Norrie Paramor. As a producer he had several No.1s in the Singles Chart.

However the work that Rowe did with artists such as Lita Roza and Dickie Valentine counted for nothing against the charge that his unforgivable lack of perception had almost resulted in the cancellation of the Swinging Sixties. For example, he classically failed to notice any commercial potential in The Beatles.

Joe Meek was one of the most imaginative of the independent record producers.

His most famous work was The Tornados' hit 'Telstar' which became the first record by a British group to hit No. 1 in the US Hot 100. It also spent five weeks atop the UK Singles Chart, with Meek receiving an Ivor Novello Award for this production as the 'best-selling A-Side' of 1962.

His other hits included 'Don't You Rock Me Daddy-O' and 'Cumberland Gap' by Lonnie Donegan.

Joe was also producing music for films, most notably *Live It Up!*, a 1963 pop music film starring Heinz Burt, David Hemmings and Steve Marriott. He wrote most of the songs and incidental music, much of which was recorded by The Saints.

Danny mentioned The Stormers who were busy in London in the traditional clubs around 1960. They sent a demo tape to Joe Meek – who was heavily into Buddy Holly.

Meek promptly renamed the group The Outlaws.

Donegan Was Difficult

'Donegan was difficult at the best of times'
John Pilgrim

John Pilgrim was a member of The Vipers who were one of the earliest skiffle groups around, and one of the first groups to play at the 2 I's. He has very thorough memories.

'I'd begun with The City Ramblers and Russ and I had fallen out with them – something that's long forgotten. So I was looking around for places to play.

Remember at that time we were not skilled musicians. This was 1954, I think and it's when I really started to learn to play, which is what we all wanted.

Soho was such an informal place then. You could hire a room for rehearsal for about £7, put a few chairs in and charge half a crown admission – and in people would come.

Wally Whyton and Johnny Booker were mentors of the 2 I's and they had all sorts of people sitting in – I remember Dis Dizley, Tommy of course, and Davey Graham.

Talking of Dis, I do remember George Melly saying of him, "He was unbelievably generous when he had some money, and unbelievably predatory when he hadn't."

I was just out of the army so I guess it was about 1954–55 and we just got together and formed The Vipers.

I remember a guy called Johnny York who fancied himself as a super manager, bringing Lonnie Donegan down.

What nobody realized was that Donegan and I had a long-term feud from my "going into the army" party in 1948.

At the party Marty Feldman had upset Donegan greatly – I then happened to mention to Donegan that I had none of his records. He went potty! So even before The Vipers got a big name I got the sack for being rude to Donegan.

But Donegan was difficult at the best of times.

What happened then was that Jean Van den Bosch – a very good singer – said that he and the others were at the 2 I's and needed a washboard player – the BBC were coming down to film them – so in I went and more or less stayed with them.

They made a half-hour film, but on the night it was to be shown the news was full of the Russian invasion of Hungary. This was 23rd October 1956 so we got about five minutes.

We got so popular that Ray Hunter the I's manager started us doing two sets a night. But you know we thought of ourselves as folk musicians – we didn't know enough to play jazz – which we all liked.

When our first record "Pick a Bale of Cotton" went into the Top 10 we started playing at the Prince of Wales Theatre on the edge of Piccadilly Circus. After the show was over we used to run back to the I's to do our set.

I remember Soho as a village in those days with several different communities. It was London's Greenwich Village and pretty harmless – that's before Westminster Council stepped in and sold off all the leases. Before that nobody made any real money but everybody was happy.

It was genuine entertainment that did not include drugs, or sex, or crime. It was not a gay area of course in those days, except for dear Quentin Crisp who was a lovely man. We all called him Mr. Crisp and we all loved him.

The Vipers were in the club one night and we were singing "Don't You Rock Me Daddy-O". I remember Donegan came down with a copy-taker and stole it from us. He was a thieving bastard. He never wrote anything – he copyrighted everything that was already in the public domain.

He was credited with "I'll Never Fall in Love Again", which Presley recorded but in fact, it was the folk song "Wandering" which Johnny Booker had recorded years before. The trouble was that George Martin wouldn't release it as a single – the silly bugger.

But The Vipers were the first group to break through at a good level. We were surprised when we became popular – we only expected a small cult following.

There were several proper clubs in Soho and, if you got into one you were considered to have "made it".

I met Dylan Thomas at The Mandrake – that place had several rooms, each with different music. Anyway, one night there was this great fat drunk man at the bar and he turned round to me and asked if I was Welsh. When I said no he replied, "Thank fuck for that, what would you like to drink?"

Thomas had a reputation of never having any money and, quite literally, they turned him upside-down one night to see if change fell out of his pockets.

There was one coffee house I do remember called Frenches, and you could get your mail addressed there – so I used to write to myself and then go in and say in a loud voice, "Any mail for me?"

In the end I didn't come back to the 2 I's when it became a rock 'n' roll venue.'

Quentin Crisp, who died in 1999, was born Denis Charles Pratt. He was an English writer, artist's model, actor and raconteur known for his memorable and insightful witticisms. He became a gay icon in the 1970s after the publication of his memoir, *The Naked Civil Servant*.

It brought to the attention of the general public his defiant exhibitionism and long-standing refusal to remain in the closet. Actor John Hurt won the Bafta Best Actor award for the 1975 Thames Television film, based on Crisp's memoirs, which were first published in 1968.

The Naked Civil Servant documented Crisp's troubles when he refused to hide his homosexuality and lifestyle during a time when being gay was illegal in Britain.

The film was placed fourth in a poll by industry professionals to find the 100 Greatest British Television Programmes of the twentieth century.

John recalled The Mandrake Club. It was in Meard Street and comprised a series of basement rooms. It was frequented by many jazz musicians mainly because of its ambience and also because of the restaurant.

It stayed open very late and the music was continued until the early hours of the morning by the legendary singer, pianist and entertainer, Cab Kaye.

The founder and original owner was Boris, a Soho character of Russian origin who started a chess club in the basement of one of the once-stately terraces that lined the tiny street.

It was a club where your anonymity was sacrosanct.

Ronnie Scott was a regular visitor; his girlfriend Sue, worked behind the bar.

John mentioned Wally Whyton but it was Wally's wife, Mary, who in one way changed pop culture. She invented the 'hand jive'.

The space in the 2 I's was so small – and on many occasions so packed that there was no room to dance. So she and four or five others developed the routine while sitting rather squashed together. Well, there you go! Another valuable piece of information for your next pub quiz.

They Rescued Us

'The British army trucks were around so they rescued us'
Hylda Simms

John Pilgrim spoke of The City Ramblers. They were more of a jug band – and as such had a more varied repertoire and also did more instrumentals.

John had started in the Skiffle Cellar together with Hylda Simms and her husband, having rented a room in their house in Waterloo.

Russell Quaye and The City Ramblers with Hylda Simms opened the Skiffle Cellar in Greek Street in 1957. Russell and Hylda had an open house policy where the experimental, 'give it a go feeling' of skiffle's heroic days was maintained. The Cellar lasted about three years but its reputation and style outlived it.

Hylda has very clear memories.

'At that time I was interested in folk music and used to play around the coffee bars – I also sang in a youth choir – so music was important to me, and of course I knew my way round it. The theory, I mean.

At that time skiffle was just starting with Ken Colyer and Chris Barber – although it wasn't called skiffle at that point. Anyway, we really got into it and used to play a lot in the street by Waterloo Station, usually earning more money than you would on dates.

Later on we decided to open a club – "The City Ramblers" at the Princess Louise pub. It was the first club to be opened and it was very successful.

It's amazing, when you look back at how things happen. While we were playing at Waterloo Station we were "discovered" by a German agent Klaus Baronbrook who offered us a tour of Germany. Remember, the war was still very fresh in people's minds, so we hesitated – then thought, great – let's go for it! The City Ramblers sort of funded our trip.

We bought an old London ambulance and painted it up and off we went to the continent. This was 1956 so it was a real adventure.

Plus it was tough for me at the beginning, because I was pregnant.

On one occasion we had to go to Berlin, which meant going through the East German corridor. Unfortunately we took a wrong turn did a lot of unnecessary miles and ran out of petrol. However, fortunately for us the British army trucks were about and they rescued us.

After we came back to England we realized that skiffle had become the big thing – the hit parade – everything – because of "Rock Island Line".

We were contacted by Moss Empires and toured with them for a while.

We always took part in the Soho Fair, dressing up and going through the streets and singing.

I never actually played at the 2 I's but went there on several occasions.

Of course there were the girls in Soho I remember – always the same ones in the same doorway. There was one who lived upstairs; I think her name was Angie and I know some of the hornier band members used to pop up and see her now and again.

The area was very international and I think it was the only place in London where you could buy foreign newspapers at that time.'

The Princess Louise pub is still there and going strong.

Its classic Victorian interior is still gloriously intact. Indeed after a recent refurbishment, it's come back with extra period additions, with partitions now running down the sides of the island bar, creating the sort of subdivided drinking spaces common in nineteenth-century gin palaces.

Moss Empires was a British company formed from the merger of the theatre empires owned by Sir Edward Moss and Sir Oswald Stoll in 1898. This formed the largest British chain of Music halls.

The business was successful in controlling thirty-three music halls and, by 1905, almost every sizeable town in Great Britain had an Empire, or Coliseum theatre, run by Stoll, and many newly constructed and designed by Frank Matcham.

The company withdrew from promoting music hall in 1960, due to increasing competition from other entertainment media. The organization continues as a Really Useful Theatres, formed from the merger of the Stoll Moss Group with RUG Theatres, in January 2000. They continue to manage seven theatres: The London Palladium, Theatre Royal Drury Lane, the Palace, The New London, The Adelphi, Her Majesty's and The Cambridge Theatre.

Kid With the Guitar

'Make sure you give the job to the kid with the guitar'
Dave Samson

When I was eighteen, in 1960, and working at the Queen's Theatre I thought I was in a great place and time – it was total freedom – for a teenager. Others, of course, were there earlier.

One such person was Dave Samson, memories go back to 1956–58 when he was working as a messenger boy for an advertising agency in Park Lane. He recalls:

'My lunch time often saw me on the way to Soho and the I's. I used to go down and see people like Tommy Steele and Terry Dene – even during the day they were there.

It was sixpence for a expresso coffee if my memory is correct. My dad had bought me a guitar and I would go to work with it. I remember I went for a job interview for an American company who did Phillips records – which is why I wanted to join them – I thought it would be an "in".

So, I turned up for the interview and I was sitting in the reception with my guitar when this American guy asked me if I could play it. I said yes.

I found out later that he had sent word to the personnel office, "Make sure you give the job to the kid with the guitar."

Well, I did get the job and he helped me a lot. There was also a lady called Beryl at Phillips who gave a me a lot of advice on how to play my guitar and which chords to learn first.

Later I joined a group with Martin Murray from The Honeycombs. We all came from Chingford and that was our first group.

I used to go to Lancaster Gate and busk on a Thursday and Friday night and make as much as £7 a night, which was a lot of money in those days. By nine o'clock I'd finish and then go to the 2 I's, get my frothy coffee and go downstairs, and there would be people like Tony Sheriden and Brian Bennett. Often Hank and Bruce would be there too, plus many others.

When you look at what many of these people have achieved – it was quite a gathering.

I remember on one occasion getting on the tube – about 1958 I think it was, and this guy got on with carrot-coloured hair, which in those days was really freaky! It was the first time I saw Wee Willie Harris but within six months we were working together.

On another occasion I was in Spain for a holiday – it was a long way in those days – and I got a letter from my mum. A letter had come from Norman Sheffield who wanted me to join the band. When I came home I went for an audition in a studio on the Great Cambridge Road – and that's basically how I got into The Hunters.

One of my great friends was Billy Fury – a complete nutter – a lovely guy and a great animal lover.

I remember once we were driving to Bath for a gig – Tommy Bruce was driving when suddenly Billy shouted, "STOP".

"What's up?" Tommy asked. There was an injured bird in the gutter flapping its wings. We had to pull over, pick it up and drive to the PDSA in Bath.

"We'll be late for the gig," we protested.

"Bugger the gig" said Billy, "This little creature needs help." That's a good memory.

In 1959 I wrote "Sweet Dreams" and made a demo of it and went to Cliff's house and asked him to do me a favour and just listen to it.

He got on his scooter took the demo disc to Norrie Paramor. A couple of hours later he came back, put it on the table and simply said "Norrie wanted me to do it but he thinks your voice is better."

With the 2 I's you cannot ever explain the atmosphere – at the time you had no idea what was happening.

Soho itself was a shady area but you wouldn't have wanted it any other way. It certainly had a bit of a reputation in those days for being a bit strange – it was only just opening up. You got off the tube at Tottenham Court Road and walked through Soho square and you really got a buzz.'

*   *   *

Norman and Barry Sheffield started the Trident Studios at 17 St. Anne's Court, Soho.

They recorded several big hits with artists like Manfred Mann and David Bowie.

With The Hunters, Dave made five singles and an EP in the early 1960s that were very much in the Cliff Richard and The Shadows mould. Similar, if you like, to the tamer elements of Elvis Presley and Ricky Nelson.

The Honeycombs group's founder Martin Murray had worked as a hairdresser, with Honey Lantree as his assistant. They decided to combine his profession with the name of the drummer, and changed their name to The Honeycombs. Hence their most distinguishing mark was their female drummer, Honey Lantree. The Honeycombs' first recording 'Have I The Right?' hit No. 1 in the UK and No. 5 in the US in the autumn of 1964, shortly after the start of the British invasion in pop music.

It was Joe Meek's final hit in the United States.

Origin of the Ankle Chain

'I wonder if girls today understand the origin of the ankle chain'
Wee Willie Harris

Dave Samson mentioned Wee Willie Harris who, in fact, lived in Bermondsey only a couple of streets away from Tommy Steele before he moved into the flat above the I's. Wee Willie Harris recalls:

'The first I knew about the 2 I's was when I saw it in the paper – so I went down to see what was going on.

I had been working for Martini up to that time but had been given the sack. I ended up at the I's serving coffee for a couple of quid. That's around 1956, early 1957.

Originally I was Charlie Harris but when I became Wee Willie I lived alone above the coffee bar for about four years – then went up to Manchester.

When I was in Bermondsey I was a bit under 18 – and with friends we used to go to the New Cross Palais. In those days there was no music in the interval so I asked if I could get up and do a couple of numbers. The answer was a big Yes . . .

This was fine for a few weeks, then one Saturday night the manager said no. Apparently he had some agents coming in to see the kid, Tommy of course, and I remember he did "Rock with the Caveman" and "Elevator Rock".

When I first recorded "Rockin at the 2 I's" it went straight onto the juke box at the I's and a lot of people played it.

The coffee bar scene was a huge influence on the British rock 'n' roll development in the early fifties.

Soho was always an interesting place – from many different points of view. What I do remember about the area were the girls . . . There was always the same girl in the same doorway and we used to talk to one or two of them. I do remember that if they had a chain on their left ankle they were "business". It was a sort of ID. I often wonder if girls today who wear chains just as jewellery really understand the origin of the ankle chain.

On one occasion Lionel Bart asked me to audition for "Oliver". He wanted me to do the "Artful Dodger" so I sang "Any Old iron". He said 'Willie, I would love to use you but you look a bit too old" – so I turned round and said in my best Jewishy accent, "Well, I could do Fagin, my life."

Of course, at one time I had my hair dyed pink – at the suggestion of Paul Lincoln – and I remember walking through the West End and getting builders whistling at me. God knows what they thought. Bit different today isn't it?

Looking back, I suppose I was an exception to the rule, dying my hair all manner of colours and wearing larger-than-life stage jackets that looked like the coat hanger was still inside. I had tight drainpipe trousers, and a huge polka-dot bow tie. I understandably stood out from the rest of the pack.

Of course I had a love for hard American rock 'n' roll and seemed able to perform it with unrelenting energy. It kept me working and recording from the mid 1950s basically to today, working everything from nostalgia packages to cruise ships across the Atlantic.'

Willie was resident pianist at the 2 I's and, as he told me, just about anyone who was anyone played there.

When Lionel Bart took on Charles Dickens as a musical, he had no plans to be reverential. After all, this was a man who, unsatisfied with his real surname, Begleiter, had changed it on a whim after passing the London hospital, St. Bartholomew's, on a bus.

At twenty-nine, he had already written hit songs for Tommy Steele and Cliff Richard, and collaborated with theatrical icon Joan Littlewood on a musical called *Fings Ain't Wot They Used T'Be*.

Now he wanted to try something heftier. Despite his track record, twelve London managements rejected the chance to buy the rights to *Oliver!*

Finally, Donald Albery, running the New Theatre later renamed for him, agreed to stage the whole shebang for £15,000. During the run the Artful Dodger was played by a number of actors including Tony Robinson and David Jones.

In 1957 a sixteen-year-old boy was arrested for busking in Wardour Street. Can you believe that! Apparently he was 'disturbing the peace' His name? (Long) John Baldry.

Coincidentally, his father was a London policeman and the story goes that he did not bail him out, but let young John spend the night in the cell.

When he was seventeen he was trying his luck at the various bars in the area, which included the Gyre & Gimble and the Blues and Barrel House Club, which was held at the Roundhouse.

After he had begun to visit the Gyre & Gimble his policeman dad paid a visit – and apparently was none too happy about what he saw. However to the benefit of us all and the music industry young John stuck to his guns.

John Baldry grew to a towering 6 ft 7 in, which gave rise to the nickname 'Long' John.

Gifted with a deep, rich voice, he was one of the first British vocalists to sing blues music in clubs.

In and around the early 1960s, he sang with Alexis Korner's band Blues Incorporated, with whom he recorded the first British blues album in 1962, 'R&B at the Marquee'.

The Gyre & Gimble, which was just off Villiers Street in Charing Cross, had always had a guitar club and those appearing included Dis Dizley, Jean Van den Bosch, Tommy Steele and Johnny Booker – it served, in fact, as Booker's headquarters. Subsequently, it became the centre of skiffle folk, ballad and rock input.

And the rest, as they say, is history.

About three years before he died I recorded an interview with Ronnie Scott who told me about Albert Dimes, who at one time was the area 'Godfather'.

I was with Ronnie in his club in Frith Street. On a shelf behind his desk was a very dusty looking Magnum of Champagne. When I asked him if it was an advertising 'dummy' bottle he assured me it was real.

Apparently, when he first moved into the premises in Frith Street, Albert Dimes, who knew both Ronnie and his father gave them the bottle. They were told not to open it until the club was out of the red. As far as I know it is still there.

Dimes was an Anglo-Italian who grew up in 'Little Italy'. Initially he was a racecourse conman who later went into business with Frankie Fraser and Eddie Richardson supplying fruit machines to night clubs.

During the 1950s the local rackets – illegal gambling, extortion and protection – were run by the likes of Jack Spot, Billy Hill and Albert Dimes.

These people had their fingers in a number of pies from the organized criminal activities just mentioned to 'smash and grab raids'. Armed robberies were on the increase at that time, while prostitution and vice were concentrated in the hands of the Maltese family, the Messina brothers.

In a sense, Dimes calmed the gang warfare in the area becoming a peacemaker between rival gangs.

Like many criminals of the period Albert got to know several people in the film and television world. Indeed, on one occasion he was consulted for a film made in 1960 – *The Criminal* – by Joseph Losey.

Cancer caught up with Albert Dimes in 1972 and his funeral was attended by, amongst others, the actor Stanley Baker.

Ronnie Scott's playing was much admired on both sides of the Atlantic. Charles Mingus said of him in 1961: 'Of the white boys, Ronnie Scott gets closer to the negro blues feeling; the way Zoot Sims does.'

Scott is perhaps best remembered for co-founding, with former tenor sax player Pete King, The Ronnie Scott's Jazz Club, which opened on 30th October 1959 in a basement at 39 Gerrard Street in Soho, later moving to a larger venue nearby at 47 Frith Street in 1965.

Scott regularly acted as the club's genial Master of Ceremonies, and was famous for his repertoire of jokes, asides and one-liners. A typical introduction might go:

'Our next guest is one of the finest musicians in the country. Unfortunately in the city, he's crap.'

After 1963, many restrictions were eased on exchange of artists with the USA, and therefore many clubs prospered after that period. The Flamingo and Ronnie Scott's were even more successful with the arrival of major US names.

That Guy is a Fag

'Hey man, do you think that guy is a fag?'
Terry Dene

Prior to his music career Terry Dene worked in the HMV record store in Oxford Street. He recalls:

'When I was still working at the HMV store we used to get all the new releases and I recall the first Presley disc and I thought – yes, that's what I want to do.

There I met Brian Gregg who became my bass player. He said to me one day "Why don't you come to Soho?"

I was young so I was shocked and nervous and I remember saying something like "Don't gangsters go there?"

He assured me it was not as bad as that and you could get a good cup of coffee for sixpence. We went and I started making friends and singing the odd bit in the I's. After a few weeks Paul Lincoln asked me to be sure to be there at the end of the week as he had some agents coming down.

The bar itself was cramped to say the least – just inside the door there was a juke box which hammered out stuff like "Blueberry Hill" and "A Whole Lotta Shakin' Goin' On". I remember there was a Gaggia coffee machine and high stools around the bar.

There was a guy who worked there I remember called Big Roy – he weighed about 32 stone. He used to help out in security.

One night we were in the sister club in Gerrard Street and there were a few of us. Tommy Steele and I were discussing names – I was just starting up at that time and trying to decide on a name – things like "Terry Wills and the Woodbines", and Mickie Most turned and suggested Dean. I said yes, but I'll change the spelling to Dene.

Suddenly there was this huge banging and shouting. Apparently there was a gang with axes and clubs outside trying to get into the club and I remember Big Roy just stood behind the door so they could not open it. Well, he was heavy.

I particularly remember some of the guys that also played there including Tommy, although I don't think he actually played there much. Then there was Chas, of course, and The Vipers – oh, and you did not forget Wee Willie Harris.

There were a lot of "arty" businesses springing up in the area, alongside a few older and well-established businesses.

There was an agency for film extras in Archer Street and many of us used to go and try and get some work. Myself and Mickie Most got a day filming for *Saint Joan* – I think we got £3.50 per day. We were broke so we stayed all night on Euston Station then got on the train by hopping over the barrier without tickets.

On the set I fell asleep in one of the houses and I remember Otto Preminger was shouting at people to take their glasses off. "This is another time in history."

I was woken up by someone shouting "She's burning!"

Jean Seberg – on the set as "Joan" was actually getting singed because the wind had changed.

Anyway, it all worked out okay.

The day finished and we all went back on the train – without tickets. Mickie had the idea that if we walked backwards off the train and up the platform as if we were seeing somebody off, to the barrier at Waterloo we would get away with it. Sounds crazy – but it worked.

I remember on another occasion I was with Eddie Cochran and Gene Vincent and we went to Larry Parnes' place for a drink. Larry had gone out of the room and Eddy turned to us and said "Hey man, do you think that guy is a fag?"

We did a Christmas concert at work and most of the executives got drunk – I did a number helped by one of the sale assistants who played drums, with Brian Gregg at that time on harmonica. The executives didn't take much notice, but later when I was discovered they said – "Why didn't we get you signed?" and I said "Well, you had your chance, but you ignored me."'

In June 1957, Terry Dene was the biggest name on board the 'Rock across The Channel' trip. This was a Rock 'n' roll day trip to Calais and back; a bit more on that later.

Brian Gregg had been a professional bass player for eight or nine years then, having joined his first professional band Les Hobeaux around 1958. He was also in a band with Tommy Steele and used to play the bass guitar for The Vipers and The Blue Flames.

By Selling Kisses

'Our girlfriends made more by selling kisses'
Johnny D'Avensac

The Johnny Makins Skiffle Group was an early band. An original member was Johnny D'Avensac, who recalls:

'There was a guy called Tex Makins (Tony). We went to school together and we started going to jazz clubs and saw people like the Crane River Jazzmen; also the Sonny Morris Jazzmen at the Ken Colyer club.

Every interval this guy called Chas McDevitt would get up and do very good skiffle – without Nancy Whiskey I remember.

Tony and I reckoned we could do skiffle – so we said to each other – how about it?

The first instrument I bought was a banjo and I tried to emulate Chas. Didn't do too well, but we tried and tried.

Tex actually made himself an Apple Barrel bass, so after a few lessons with a guy who could actually play, I bought myself a guitar and we started doing a little skiffle.

We started busking around the area and actually did okay, even though I only knew about three chords.

So off we went again and found a guy called Johnny Moreton, who really could play.

So The Johnny Makins Skiffle Group was created and of course we wanted to get known so we started busking theatre queues and used to make about £3 each – which was a lot of money in those days. And that was every night! Our girlfriends made more – by selling kisses!

We soon gained confidence and decided to have a go in a club.

At first we played intervals in Cy Laurie's Jazz Club then we went down to the 2 I's. The place was always packed.

It was an emerging place and there were loads of guys down there with guitars and always a lot of people watching – and we played our hearts out. We were asked to join The Vipers – we would sing, we would harmonize and eventually, we would all be in tune!

Week after week we'd go back to the I's and eventually we were asked to do a couple of sessions at the magnificent sum of 15 shillings per night each, which was nothing compared to busking.

I remember the 2 I's so very vividly – it was just as Terry Dene has said. It was a place every one wanted to go to – it was always packed.'

Cy Laurie was a clarinettist, bandleader and an important figure in the British revivalist jazz movement. He began playing soprano saxophone, which had been left at a pawnbroker's shop owned by his father. By the late 1940s the revival, or rediscovery, of early jazz was gathering momentum and Laurie took an enthusiastic part.

One of its centres was Cy Laurie's Jazz Club, held nightly at Mac's Rehearsal Rooms in Great Windmill Street.

There was a night club on the ground floor and a boxing gym above. Dark and intimate, with a dance floor surrounded by dilapidated sofas, these premises held an irresistible bohemian appeal for the young people from the suburbs who flocked to the club's night-long jam sessions.

Laurie led the resident band. When playing, he tended to get carried away, waving his instrument wildly in the air. 'If you played trumpet or trombone on either side of him you stood to get badly cut about unless nimble,' observed his fellow clarinettist and rival bandleader Sandy Brown.

Cy Laurie died aged 75.

You Could Never Really Hear the Words

'Song? Well, you never could really hear the words'
Clive Stuart

Clive Stuart – writer and Community liaison officer – spent much of his youth in London. He recalls:

'It was an experience of a lifetime!

In early 1958, as a fourteen-year old, there was not a lot to do apart from playing cricket in the summer and football in the winter on Parliament Hill Fields.

One day my mates told me of a place in Soho where you could see the current rock 'n' roll bands, in a great atmosphere and more importantly, at little cost – not even five bob (25p)!

There was never a suggestion that it would be unsafe or drugs would be sold, and even the sale of alcohol was never mentioned. So, without my parents' permission, one night I jumped on a trolley bus which stopped off at Tottenham Court Road.

I began walking down Charing Cross Road looking for Old Compton Street which was, in fact, on my right.

At the 2 I's, from the outside, it was an ordinary coffee shop. There was not a feeling of any unusual activities when you went through the door. On the left was the counter where frothy coffee was sold, if I remember correctly at 2s 3d, (11p) and then you either sat on a stall on the right, or leaned against the wall, and rested your cup, saucer and spoon on a small shelf.

In those days it was not considered necessary to have the spoon on a string. That was later when "memorabilia items from 2 I's" were in great demand.

Okay, maybe I did not have to buy a coffee, but it seemed the right thing to do as a sort of entry fee as far as I was concerned.

I think later on in years to come there may have been a charge, but this was the early days of the 2 I's.

The cup and saucer were pyrex, sugar was in square lumps or you helped yourself from a large container with a plastic spout – which occasionally people used to unscrew and then add salt. My brother used to do that as his joke. These containers can still be seen today in roadside cafés.

So, having drunk your coffee, which was not compulsory as many just left them on the counter, you followed the crowd to a door, which led to a narrow and steep staircase. It was not only the claustrophobic atmosphere that hit you, due to – it seemed hundreds but was probably only forty or so – people jumping up and down, but also the noise was deafening!

It took some time it seemed minutes, but was only a moment or two, to see what was going on and also where to stand. You had to move somewhere, otherwise the people on the stairs behind you would be prevented from entering the cellars.

The Cavern in Liverpool had not been thought about at that time!

Once acclimatizing to the feel of where you were, it was best if you found a space to stand and look at the bands. People may have trodden on your toes, or you did that to others, but there was no need to apologise, as you could not be heard anyway!

No Master of Ceremonies, no introductions, just one band after the other.

I remember Wee Willie Harris; he played the piano, and in fact was one of the resident performers for some time. He was an extraordinary man, very active and would leap all over the small stage whenever he could, which was limited as he was mostly playing at the time!

However, in the early sixties there was one person I do remember, who stood out more than any other at the time.

It was Screaming Lord Sutch. He wore a bowler hat – no room above his head for a top hat, and then when he took it off, he would wave his very long hair round and round to the sounds of the amazing lead guitarists interpretation of the "song". Song? Well, you could never really hear the words, and no one sang along!

It can be read on this late performers' website that in fact, what I must have been watching was him in an audition for local agents. He may only have appeared once, and was given a UK tour shortly afterwards!

Although Cliff Richard and Adam Faith did appear, it was later in the sixties and after I found other interests. It will always be my memories of the very early days of the 2 I's, which will stay with me forever!

Oh, by the way, I had to be home before 10.30 p.m. or just after – yes even at that age, as the local cinema films ended at 10.00 p.m. and my parents would not want me staying out late.'

I wonder how many of today's teenagers will look back in fifty years' time with such fond memories as we have – indeed any memories at all? It seems that all some want to do is get blind drunk, or if not are listening to things plugged into their ears most of the time and are generally oblivious of anything around them.

And without mentioning any current or recent music groups it seems to me that so many confuse volume with talent. I truly wonder how many artists of today will be around in ten years, time, let alone be remembered for years in the future.

Screaming Lord Sutch was born in Hampstead, North West London. In the 1960s, inspired by one of his favourite rock 'n' roll stars, Screaming Jay Hawkins, he changed his name to Screaming Lord Sutch, 3rd Earl of Harrow. He had a successful career in the early 1960s as a rock 'n' roll artist.

Early works included recordings produced by Joe Meek. During the 1960s, Screaming Lord Sutch was known for his horror-themed stage show, as well as for usually dressing as Jack the Ripper, pre-dating the shock-rock antics of Alice Cooper by several years.

Accompanied by his band, The Savages, he often started the show by coming out of a big black coffin. Other stage props included knives and daggers, skulls, and 'bodies'.

Although he did not regard himself as 'talented' he released many horror themed singles during the early- to mid-1960s, the most popular and well known of which was 'Jack the Ripper'.

The Soho Fair

On 14th July 1956, which was Bastille Day, Soho came alive with the Soho Fair, an inspiration of the landlord of the York Minster in Dean Street. For one week in July this festival brought an abundance of colour and excitement to the area.

The Soho Fair, generally recognized as Britain's first 'pop' festival of any significance took place in and around Old Compton Street.

Comprising of a parade of half a dozen top skiffle groups, the fair culminated in a set by ace skifflers, The Vipers, outside the 2 I's coffee bar, an event that would help establish the 2 I's as *the* pivotal venue in the evolution of early British pop and rock 'n' roll.

Ron Gould recalled that for people who were well known or lived in the close vicinity, an advantage was that you were allowed to become a salesman for the Soho Fair programme on which you made quite a nice profit.

'I had the most profitable site' recalls Ron, 'which was on the corner of Old Compton Street and Wardour Street'.

One of the main events was the waiters' race, with more than seventy of them running in full uniform – which ranged from evening dress to native far eastern costume, depending upon their place of work.

It began with a circuit of Soho Square and ended at the corner of Frith Street and Old Compton Street. Each of the runners had to carry a tray with a half bottle of bubbly and two glasses – and of course, not drop anything.

The winner that year was Robert Taylor from the Catford Café and the second was Toni Rigotti from a restaurant in Greek Street.

As the crowds descended into Old Compton Street there was a shout of 'Fire!'

Smoke was detected in the kitchen of a café – apparently the parson's nose of a chicken was on fire!

The fire brigade were called but had great problems – Old Compton Street is not wide and there were vehicles parked on both sides of the road – plus of course the crowds. Anyway all was sorted out and little damage was done.

Chas McDevitt who was busking during the period remembers the fair.

'With Redd Sullivan on vocals the band would set up in a doorway. Redd would start singing and after a few minutes Adam would "bottle up" and we would move on to another pitch.' Because it was the week of the fair they were not treated as (Long) John Baldry had been but were left alone by the police.

The following year one of the more adventurous events organized by the 2 I's was a no-passport trip to France. This was in June 1957.

It was Paul Lincoln who came up with the idea of organizing the trip, which would run from Southend to Calais, France.

He rented an old paddle steamer called SS *Royal Daffodil*. It was a boat that had previously been hit by a German bomb as she played her part in the evacuation of Dunkirk during the Second World War.

'Rock Across the Channel' featured several of the bands of the day including Rory Blackwell's Blackjacks and Lo Don's Ravin Rockers.

The paddle steamer sailed from Gravesend across the channel and punters paid the huge sum of £2.

Ron Gould told me that they planned to be on deck and sing 'The Marseillaise' as they arrived in Calais.

Well, to be precise it was supposed to be Terry Dene – the biggest name – and Wee Willie Harris. In reality they did not know it so Ron ended up singing it with Russell Quay.

The ship was welcomed by the mayor of Calais and the town band.

The cross channel rock 'n' roll trips continued until 1963 when, according to legend, a promoter ran off with the money.

Sadly the Soho Fair was not to become an institution. By 1961 it was at an end and the Soho association for the fair was discontinued. The attendance at a meeting to discuss the next event was so low that Ron Smith, a member of the association council was quoted as saying,

'There was nothing we could do but to decide to wind it up. There is such a lack of interest.'

So in 1961 out went the fair and in came parking meters. To be precise 550 of them were installed to deal with the parking problems in the area.

This was on top of the Street Offences Act, the new rules about gambling, and the prospect of finding a way around the new licensing laws.

All this was to prove hard going – at least in the short term – for the restaurants, theatre goers and strip club watchers. So whereas before you could drive in any direction around Soho, suddenly you had to know where you were going in order not to go the wrong way down a one way street. But actually it makes sense because of the increase in traffic and the narrowness of the streets.

Looking Up My Petticoats

'While I was dancing the camera was on the floor looking up at my
petticoats'
Christine Runicles

When I was planning – and talking about this book – a good friend
and fellow member of an acting group based at the Mercury Theatre,
Colchester, Christine Runicles exclaimed, 'Oh, the 2 I's – I used to work
there.'

What a small world it is – so of course I asked what her recollections
were.

'I first went to the 2 I's with my friend Brenda in early 1957, having
started work in a bank. We had seen a skiffle group playing in one of
the nearby clubs and thought it exciting. She did not like the crowded
atmosphere but I loved it because everyone was so friendly and looked
out for each other.

I would go as often as I could – straight from work. Later in the
evening someone would always take me to Charing Cross station for my
train to Upminster.

When I started going Tommy Steele was moving on to better things
and Les Hobeaux had just got the top act. There was Les Bennetts,
Darrel Lyte and Roy Tobin as guitarists, Keith Larner and Roger Smith
as vocalists and later on Brian Gregg on tea chest.

I still have pictures of them signed by Les and photos of the 2 I's.
Les Bennetts soon became my special friend and used to borrow my
Hofner guitar which he electrified when he needed it for recording. He
also visited my home when he had a few days off.

I spent hours down in the cellar listening to their music. It got very
hot down there but I remember there was a small hatch so if anyone

fainted you could just about squeeze them out to the street for air.

I started to help behind the bar making frothy coffees and we also used to sell delicious rumbabas and apple strudels.

One day the BBC cameras came in and I remember the East End comedians Mike and Bernie Winters and Bernie's St. Bernard dog Schnorbitz were there.

I made many friends in that time, some of whom went on to be big stars. I remember Adam Faith, or Terry as I knew him, Mickie Most, Vince Eager, and Wee Willie Harris who I saw on stage many times with Marty Wilde.

We all used to go by coach to other venues and I can remember sitting on Marty Wilde's lap because there were no seats left on the coach.

I used to spend a lot of time with Colin Hicks, (Tommy Steele's brother) girlfriend and one day Jack Good was looking for some extras to appear in the *Six-Five Special* film they were making. We had already appeared on several *Six-Five* BBC specials which, incidentally, replaced the hour shut down between 6 and 7 p.m. so people could get their children to bed.

The series featured Don Lang and the Frantic Five with Pete Murray. We thought it would be fun to take part in a film and took a couple of unauthorized days off work, but of course we got found out.

Never mind, it was exciting and I remember we all went on strike as they weren't going to pay us, but after refusing to cooperate they relented.

Don Lang was supposed to be in the film, but in the end Lonnie Donegan took over together with Petula Clark, Jim Dale, Cleo Lane and Johnny Dankworth.

Cleo and Johnny were a couple and were really lovely. We had to sit on a train doing hand jive to "The Six-Five Specials Coming Down the Line". Then we danced rock 'n' roll. I had a very pretty petticoat on made by my mum so, whilst I was dancing, the camera was on the floor showing all the colourful layers going round and round. My chance of fame!

I never saw the finished film but it was a great time to be a teenager.'

The *Six-Five Special* Chris mentioned was first broadcast from the 2 I's on 16th November 1957.

It was a British television programme launched when both television and rock 'n' roll were in their infancy in Britain. It was the BBC's first attempt at a rock 'n' roll programme, an innovation and much imitated, even today. It was called *Six-Five Special* because of the time it was broadcast – it went out live at five past six on Saturday evenings.

Highlights of the show included Terry Dene, although his slot was filmed elsewhere.

That first show also brought attention to someone called Terry Nelhams, later to be known as Adam Faith.

Jack Good was the producer and disc jockey Pete Murray was its presenter, using the catchphrase 'Time to jive on the old six-five'.

The resident band, Lord Rockingham's XI had a UK no. 1 instrumental in November 1958 with 'Hoots Mon'.

The show was scheduled to last six weeks but, as a result of Jack Good ignoring guidance given by the BBC not to show the young audience alongside performers, it continued indefinitely.

Chris mentioned Mike and Bernie. They won a talent contest held in Manchester and the first prize which was a one-week tour.

On 25th June 1955 Mike and Bernie appeared for the first time on television, on the BBC show called *Variety Parade*. The show was an undoubted hit for both the BBC and the act. The brothers remained with the show until 1958.

Soon they appeared on *Sunday Night At The London Palladium*, which was a very popular show in its day.

Now Piss Off

'Cos she's my sister, now piss off'
Ed Pearson

Performers changed names almost as often as their shirts. Ed Pearson was in those days known as Eddie Pierce.

'My memories are of the great days in Soho playing at the cellar with Russell Quaye and The City Ramblers spasm band, and Rambling Jack Elliott and Deryl Adams from the USA who would come over and tour riding on a vespa scooter.

One of my great friends was Steve Benbow, a great singer and guitarist, and Wally Whyton who would come down with his mates Dick Bishop and Mark Sharrett, who was the best washboard player at that time.

Another guy who would visit was a singer-songwriter by the name of Kris Kristofferson, who at the time was managed by Paul Lincoln, and he couldn't get any work.

Who would believe that now?

It was such a good time to be in Soho. I remember going busking in Soho Square with Jimmy McGregor from The City Ramblers and getting 20 quid in an hour when the fair was on.

I was known as Eddie Pierce in those days. I saw an old *Melody Maker* a while back which had an ad for the cellar with my name. Oh, happy days.

One particular story comes to mind.

The Skiffle Cellar was a basement club, and the flat above was rented by one lady of the night whose name was Sally and she would hang about outside on the pavement.

We all knew her and would greet her with a "Hi, how's biz" or whatever. She would always respond with a smile and a nod. One evening, there was a bit of a row going on so we went up to see what it was all about.

There was a copper having a row with Rambling Jack Elliott because he had parked his vespa on the pavement outside her door. The men looking for a bit of company wouldn't get there because they had to cross the street to pass, and she lost her bit of biz. The outcome was he had to park up the road. When he came back he asked the copper why he had to move, and was told quite sharply "Cos she's my sister, now piss off.'"

Ed started his music career in the 1960s in Country music. He was a founder member of the Ned Porridge Band. Over the years he toured extensively and is currently with the band Slim Pickins, performing a very successful country and comedy evening.

Steve Benbow was a British folk guitar player, singer and music director who was influential in the English folk music revival of the 1960s. He was regarded by many as a seminal influence on a whole generation.

While he was doing his National Service he learnt the guitar and quickly gained popularity entertaining the troops, including appearances on forces radio where he reputedly sang songs in eight languages.

He played traditional jazz with Dave Kier's jazz band and began accompanying some of the emerging British folk singers such as Ewan MacColl and A. L. Lloyd.

His solo recording began in 1957 when he recorded two albums: 'Steve Benbow Sings English Folk Songs' and 'Steve Benbow Sings American Folk Songs.' He went on to record over twenty albums.

He was a successful broadcaster, especially during the 1950s, appearing on *'Guitar Club, Saturday Skiffle Club* and *Easy Beat,* all popular radio shows

We Had a Hard Time

'That was 1957 and we had a hard time'
Brian 'Liquorice' Locking

It's amazing how many people easily remember those days – around the late fifties to 1960 but not so much after that. Maybe that's a common symptom of age, years back is as clear as a bell, but what did I do yesterday?

One of the long established and great musicians to attend the Plaque ceremony was Brian 'Liquorice' Locking and his memory is very clear.

'I had learnt to play several instruments, including clarinet, which has the nickname the "liquorice stick", which earned me the nickname "Liquorice".

I was in a group that went in for a skiffle competition on the telly. We came second and won £100, which was great. There were four of us, including Vince Eager. We went to the 2 I's and played down there and it so happened that the manager wanted us to play on a regular basis.

So, we all left home and lived in a hostel in Paddington. This was 1957 and we had a hard time – but it was the people that we met who helped us survive. The I's was the hub of a wheel if you like.

Vince was snapped up by Larry Parnes who managed Tommy and Marty at that time. I was going to go home but I had a call from Terry Dene who needed a bass player. So off I went to Scotland – a long way in those days. That's where I met Clem Cattini. We did an eight-week tour then went back to the I's.

Then I met Brian Bennett and we became the bass player and drummer for Tony Sheridan. So, we were a great trio backing everybody; Hank, Bruce, and all the rest. Eventually we became Vince Taylor and the Playboys.

Tony Sheridan left and was replaced by Joe Moretti – he had played on "Shakin' all over" with Johnny Kidd and the Pirates. Then Joe left and Big Jim Sullivan joined us – oh, they were great days. Eventually we teamed up with Marty and became The Wildcats.

Oh, and in 1962 I joined the Shadows, replacing Jet Harris but only stayed with them for eighteen months; my last appearance being at The London Palladium in November 1963.

I had become a Jehovah's Witness and faith was far more important to me than anything else. So I left the group so that I could devote all my time to religious activities as a Jehovah's Witness.'

Brian also provided variety to the 'Shadows sound' by occasionally playing the harmonica. His version of 'Stranger on the Shore' was a regular feature of Shadows stage performances of 1962/3, and, perhaps the best of all, his harmonica features heavily on the track 'Dakota' on the 'Sounds of the Shadows' LP.

Brian Laurence Bennett is a drummer, pianist, composer, arranger and record producer of popular music.

He was to become a regular on Jack Good's TV show *Oh Boy*. He is best known as the drummer of the British rock 'n' roll group, The Shadows. He finished school at the age of sixteen to play drums in a Ramsgate skiffle group performing for holidaymakers. After a successful period with The Wildcats, he backed Tommy Steele for some of his London stage performances.

You Are So Special

'What makes you think you are so special?'
Vince Eager

Brian 'Liquorice' Locking was in the band with Vince Eager that won a competition.

Vince remembered it well.

'It was a skiffle championship, which was televised by the BBC from a venue in Streatham.

We actually came second and won what was a fortune to us. Our band was called The Vagabonds and the following day we went to the HMV studios in Oxford Street and recorded four tracks onto an acetate disc. I think it cost us about four shillings!

Having done that we decided we would go and play at the 2 I's. The place was in my vocabulary way before I left Grantham – it just had a reputation.

For the competition we had stayed in a hotel paid for by MECCA but that was only for one night. So off we went to the YMCA. Next day we headed for the I's in the van.

We came into old Compton Street from the Cambridge Circus end and saw a long line of parked vans and cars most of which had guitars, double basses and all sorts on the roofs, sticking out of windows and boots. Remember there were no real parking restrictions in those days.

Anyway, we stopped at the back and being the tallest I was told to go into the club to see what we had to do. When I arrived it was magic; neon lights, excitement, everything. I do remember there were some really seedy looking characters about and at the door was this really big guy – he must have been about 30 stone wearing a light blue baseball jacket. I later learnt that he was known as "Big Roy".

So I went up and asked him if we could play. He said it wasn't up to him and went to speak to Tom Littlewood who came over. Tom basically told us to go to the back of the queue.

"Everyone wants to play down here; what makes you think you're so special?"

I explained that we had been on BBC television the night before and we had won second place.

"Right, bring your gear in now and get set up. By the way, what is your outfit called?"

By the time we got into the I's he had a sign up saying who we were and the TV details.

We struggled downstairs with our stuff, which was passed over the heads of the crowd who were in there. We set up, got changed and did a set for nearly an hour. It was great and went well.

The manager was obviously impressed and told everyone to leave, gave us a coffee or something then reopened and we did another set. In all, we did four that night.

After all this we were asked if we would like to do a residency at the club, which was terrific.

We went home the next day really on a high as you can imagine. We had been doing a regular Wednesday night in our home town and now we had a record so things were beginning to move.

We talked it over with our parents who basically said "give it a go". However, two of the boys were in apprenticeships so could not accept. Having got replacements we said yes and were told we would get £20 per week.

So a couple of weeks later we were back at the I's doing our stuff. We managed to get into a working men's hostel near Paddington at the princely sum of £4 2s 6d per week and this was for dinner, bed and breakfast.

The trouble was that sometimes we did not get back there until the small hours and breakfast was served really early – so we missed it. Then the evening meal was at an odd time meaning we would miss that as well, so we sometimes got really hungry.

Anyway, the end of the first week at the I's saw me in the manager's office getting what I thought was my £20. When I said I would take the others' money as well he retorted, "No that's it, £20 – for the band, not each." I can tell you, that really shocked us.

To be fair, although Tom Littlewood was a bit "mafia" he did say he would get us some extra work on Sundays with people like Tommy Steele, Terry Dene and Marty Wilde.

One night Tommy came in and Littlewood said, "This guy has a manager who will be after you, or you should talk to Mr. Lincoln who owns the I's".

The 2 I's was boosted by Jack Good when he did his live broadcast of the *Six-Five Special* from the club. What amazed everybody was how he got all the gear in the place to do the show.

Paul Lincoln and Ray Hunter were ex-wrestlers turned promoters, and they certainly bent the rules. I remember one lunchtime they were discussing some wrestling matches and saying how each fight would be rigged to ensure more money for the return match.

I never repeated what I heard to anyone for a very long time. In reality I was a little bit scared of those two so always played by the rules.

Anyway, one day I asked Paul about Sunday nights. Up to that point he had not actually seen us play. At that time there was bitter rivalry between Larry Parnes and Paul over managerial rights. Often rows would be heard from the office.

It was Larry Parnes and agent Hymie Zahl who opened the first gay club in Soho. If I remember correctly it was called the Golden Guitar. It was frequented by the early gay community, which included Russ Conway I remember.

One of the weirdest characters I recall was a stand-up comic and compere who went by the name of Zom. He was as thin as a rake because he never seemed to eat anything plus he smoked like a chimney – and not always tobacco.

About the I's though; I mean, look here, we are talking about it fifty years after the events. That says a hell of a lot. The I's truly was an institution – it was known nationally. I guess if someone had taken up a franchise – like Starbucks today, the I's would have been all over the country.

There were some great entertainers that passed through, but you know, it is like a suit that you wear for so long – then suddenly it is out of fashion and you leave it in the wardrobe. I think the same thing applies to entertainment and venues. I think the I's just outgrew itself.'

*   *   *

After the early days at the I's Vince went on to spend a lifetime in the business – and is still rocking. He was in cabaret for several years and a cruise director for more than a dozen years. He also spent time in pantomimes and a terrific five years touring the world as Elvis in *Elvis the Musical*.

In answer to my question, 'When are you going to retire?', the word 'never' was loud and clear.

Bend Down Son

'He says, bend down son and I'll make you a star'
Jay Chance

There is an old saying, 'It's not what you know but who you know'. Well, it certainly applied to Jay Chance – well sort of anyway. He remembers that it was Vince Eager who spotted him and got him a break at the 2 I's.

'My first memories take me back to when I was about fifteen. I had a guitar that my grandfather had left me and been playing for about three years.

Rock 'n' Roll was just kicking in and I heard "Peggy Sue" on a juke box in a coffee bar in Norbury. I just could not believe what I was hearing. Then I saw the film *Rock around the Clock* with this chubby little guy with a kiss curl who was okay. Then came Elvis with "Love me Tender" and, I like everyone else fell in love with him. Nothing to do with sex of course but he was just electric.

I never wanted to be a rock star but I just liked performing in front of people. I actually wanted to be a comedian but that meant finding a writer. If I sang though, I could use anybody's material.

So I became a skiffler. We were Johnny Wolf and the Wolfcubs. We began to play in parks and things. Let's face it, it was a way to get the girls – that was my prime motive.

As the months went by I was really starting to enjoy singing more than the guitar. I was at grammar school in Croydon and a friend of mine who was a year older and a prefect suggested we go to the Soho Fair. He would "bottle up" while I performed. That was 1957 and the first time I saw the 2 I's though I did not go in at that point.

One day I saw an advert in *Melody Maker*. A guy was looking for a rock 'n' roll singer to manage. I went for an audition and was taken on. He wanted to change my stage name. I had fancied the name Johnny Chance because Larry Parnes had got people with names like Eager and Wilde and I thought "Chance" kind of fitted in. He liked the surname but suggested Jay would be better. So that was that.

Then my cousin Gloria who is a little older than me suggested I go to the 2 I's.

So with a Saturday afternoon off I went feeling very nervous. I was just standing with my guitar in the I's drinking my frothy coffee very slowly and feeling very out of place.

Anyway, this guy came up to me asking if I played it and did I sing. This was mid afternoon and he took me downstairs to the very small stage and asked me to do a couple of numbers.

When I finished he said that it was good and took me upstairs to meet Tom Littlewood and asked him to give me a slot. My discoverer was Vince Eager.

So on that night I was just under sixteen years of age.

I left school and got a job in Wigmore Street with an advertising company so I could walk up to Soho and play some nights during the week. This was on top of playing every weekend for a while.

Sometimes during the evening I would work the orange machine or wash cups, then somebody would shout, "Jay, you're on." I then had to grab my guitar and fight my way through the crowd to get to the stage.

All for eighteen shillings a night. That was after Tom had taken his commission.

The thing is, I had no sense of history in the making. It was just that I did not know of any other places.

There were some interesting characters down there.

I have fond memories of Vince Taylor; he was a really nice guy. His voice was not all that good, bless him, but he could really put a song over. He had a wonderful mike technique. He would go for a high note and not quite get there but as he went for it he pulled the mike away making people think he'd made it.

Then of course there was Paul Raven, later to become Gary Glitter. It is sad the way things have turned out, but there is no doubt that he had star quality. I did a couple of gigs with him at the Condor Club in Wardour Street.

One of the local weirdos I remember was called Pinkie. He was a deaf mute and led a gang of similar people. They were minders, I think, and extremely tough but they always looked after us.

Then of course there was Larry Parnes, possibly one of the first gays I met. When the band got well established we would open with the Jerry Lee Lewis number, "I got a woman, as mean as she can be" with the words "I know a man with a long cigar, he says bend down son I'll make you a star." Larry always laughed at that.'

Jay moved on into business and later became an actor. He re-entered the mainstream music scene when his original 1960s demo records, which had been discovered in 2006, were released by Raucous Records on a CD entitled 'Rock and Roll Fever' alongside new recordings made with an updated line-up of his original backing band, The Chancellors. He appeared at the '2 I's Reunion Concert' at the 100 Club in London's Oxford Street on the 28th January 2007.

Panic Set In

'Panic set in when he suddenly screamed'
Vince Rayner

I mentioned earlier how memories seem better long term.

Evidence of that is here from guitarist Vince Rayner from Essex.

'I, like many other young people in the late fifties and sixties was lured to the 2 I's in search of fame and fortune.

I played lead guitar in a local group called Eddie Lee Cooper and the Trappers playing standard rock 'n' roll music of the time; but leaning more towards Cliff and the Drifters as they were known then.

I helped out at the Regal Theatre/Cinema, Colchester on their Sunday evening concerts and met many of the stars of the day.

On one occasion Cliff Richard was indisposed and his place on the show was taken by Vince Taylor who was unknown to me at that time. He seemed a nice young man, easy to talk to and the 2 I's came up in conversation. After promising us he would put in a good word for our group we set off one weekend in the hope of getting either an audition or just a chance to play there. We were not disappointed as although the manager on site had no idea who we were he did say we could play later that evening (no money of course).

I would often see Bruce Welch of the Shadows, who at that time were appearing at The London Palladium, standing by the juke box drinking a coke. Our first short set went well with the audience and we made several appearances over the coming months.

I remember on one occasion being asked to back by Screaming Lord Sutch who was quite alarming in those early days. Panic set in when he suddenly screamed and ran down the stairs into this tiny room wearing a large set of buffalo horns, long lank hair and an animal-skin jacket, bursting into his own version of Little Richard's "Lucille".

Like all bands who went there, payment was of little consequence. So long as we got expenses the thrill of playing in such a famous venue was all that mattered. It's still on my CV but these days I'm involved in the business as a comedian.

Some years later maybe around 1964/5 I met up again with Vince Taylor, this time in Paris where he was much more popular than in England. We went for a coffee and a chat, said our farewells and I never saw him again.

I heard a few years ago that he was no longer with us. Nice Man.

Recently, I went back to the location of the 2 I's in Old Compton Street and asked if I could look around downstairs for old times' sake. The current tenant was most helpful and when I told him that we had as many as 60–80 people down there he informed me that under Health and safety Rules he was only allowed to have 95 people on the whole of the premises, which now covers three times the area upstairs.

It brought back many happy memories and I'm glad I went back. I've since been to look at the plaque.'*

Vince is still in the business and more recently has appeared at many private functions such as Ladies' Nights on the Masonic circuit.

The BBC are still repeating many of the shows he was involved in during the 1980s and 1990s such as 'Allo 'Allo. (German General) and Hi-de-Hi (various roles).

Much of his work these days involves compering Sports Presentation Evenings where he interviews footballing celebrities who then go on to present the winning teams with their trophies.

---

* Actually, it is not health and safety that controls numbers but the occupancy factor in the Fire Regulations.

I Got Into Awful Trouble

'However, one night I got into awful trouble'
Julie Samuel

Of course, not everyone who remembers the bar was a musician.

A couple of streets away in Archer Street was the Italia Conti Drama Academy and one particularly well-known actress not only remembers it well – but also learned to hate gin.

As a child, Julie Samuel attended the Italia Conti Academy, making her professional acting debut at the age of twelve when she appeared on stage at the Victoria Palace Theatre.

But it was not all sweetness and roses.

As she told me she had been expelled from school – she did not say why – so her mother sent her to drama school.

'Actually it was sort of in the family. My grandparents had been music hall artists so I guess I caught it from them. I expect my mother thought they would tame me. Actually I had a wonderful time. It was a great school. Anyway, by the time I was thirteen I started wandering around Soho on my own.'

In answer to my question she stated it was perfectly safe – she never felt uncomfortable.

'And being a fan of rock 'n' roll – I had been for a couple of years – I happened upon the 2 I's.

So picture it. I am on my own – no one with me – I am thirteen and I just went in, sat at the bar and ordered a coffee. And the first guy I met was called Ian Samwell who used to write songs for Cliff Richard. He wasn't my type – I was not attracted to him because he was far too safe and rather normal for me. I was, after all, a bit of a rebel. However, he was sweet enough and every time we met we had a nice chat.

One day he told me he had written a song for me – it was called "High Class Baby" and he told me Cliff Richard was going to record it. You can imagine at my age what a thrill that was.

Because of my age I had to be home by ten in the evening – which meant getting a bus around nine. However one night I got into awful trouble.

Terry Dene used to be a regular together with his manager who I seem to remember was gay. Anyway, one night they asked me and a couple of girlfriends to go back to their flat for a drink.

So there we were and they asked us what we would like to drink. Well, we didn't drink – we were only about fourteen so wanting to feel grown up I said I would have a gin and orange – and my friends had the same. We probably had four – large ones. Then I remembered I had to get the Green Line bus home so we left.

So later I am sitting on the bus on my own – my friend had got off – and I am so drunk and I know I might miss my stop so I am glued to the window trying to see where to get off.

Suddenly this lady – who I realized was a friend of my mother's – helped me off the bus. I was immediately sick in the hedge and then she walked me home. I crept in and went straight to bed. As far as I know she never told my mother – and I have never touched gin since.

I saw all kinds of bands – a lot of Wee Willie Harris – he seemed to be there all the time.

I did meet Vince Taylor quite a lot – he was a bit of an oddball but had a small combo.

My sister was having her 21st birthday party and asked them if they would come and play. They said yes but she had to go and pick them up in her Mini Traveller. Guitars, amps and everything – how she got it all in I don't know.

Anyway, it turned out that they only knew three songs – all Elvis – which they played all night. They actually stayed the night camping down in the kitchen. It was a very large Edwardian house.

The guitarist slept on the floor underneath a caged mynah bird.

In the morning my sister went in and asked if he had slept okay.

"Yeah, yeah," was the answer. She then asked if the bird had kept him awake. "No, I didn't have no bird."

Later, I met Johnny Kidd and the Pirates. I met them when I was doing a pantomime. Their manager Guy Robinson decided that they needed some stage craft so we met on my first adult job in Kidderminster.'

From the age of seventeen, Julie appeared in countless films, television series and programmes and with occasional performances in theatres in London and around Britain.

After marrying the well-known assistant film director Derek Cracknell and bringing up their daughter Sarah, Julie decided to resume her acting career. She attended the London Drama Studio, where under the guidance of Peter Layton she studied drama at an advanced level, and was soon back on the boards. She went on to appear in over one hundred television shows, playing many leading roles.

These included the part of Dawn in the series *Market in Honey Lane* for a period of eighteen months. Julie was seen in six episodes of the series *The Rag Trade* and made guest appearances in *Dixon of Dock Green, Z-Cars, Emergency Ward Ten* and *Coronation Street*.

Currently she runs Loose Cannonz Ltd with song writer David Martin, to promote new musical enterprises, including young musicians, songwriters and musical shows.

In 1958, after seeing Harry Webb performing at the 2 I's Ian Samwell auditioned for and joined Webb's group as a guitarist. Shortly afterwards, the group was renamed Cliff Richard and The Drifters who later became The Shadows.

When the group won a contract with EMI's Columbia Records, Ian wrote the song, 'Move It', which was inspired by Chuck Berry. It made No. 2 on the UK Singles Chart, and is generally accepted as the first rock 'n' roll song to be written in England.

Ian played rhythm guitar on 'Move It', but was edged out of the band when Hank Marvin and Jet Harris joined. Instead, he was offered a songwriting contract, and wrote Richard's second hit single, 'High Class Baby' which Julie Samuel mentioned.

In the early 1960s he hosted lunchtime dance sessions at the Lyceum in London, using his own collection of black R&B records.

Very Rarely Buying Food

'We were mad – very rarely buying food'
Christine Ford

Christine Ford who is the same age as me was also a regular customer at the 2 I's. I wonder if we ever met.

'I was born in 1942, had a nice family and home – one of the few houses with a proper bathroom – but everything was drab and black, white or grey – no colour.

You wore two types of material, cotton or itchy wool. There were no dreams of holidays abroad. A week at Butlins was it if you were lucky – or a week in Jaywick if you were unlucky.

The only glamour was at the pictures; mostly American films, but the colours, houses, cars were all magical. The funny thing is I don't remember being envious. That was America and this was England . . .

Then came Elvis, Billy Haley, Little Richard, and we all went a little mad I think. Put this into comparison with Pearl Carr and Teddy Johnson who were very tame, it was all very wild.

Suddenly it was here; Tommy Steele, Cliff Richard, Billy Fury, Marty Wilde. And they were as good as the American singers.

The 2 I's was where it was all happening. The holy grail – you just had to go.

It was never easy for parents but ours surely never knew what hit them. Knowing it all I stormed out at seventeen and headed for the big city. I'd put my worldliness on a par with most twelve-year-olds today.

Fortunately there were plenty of jobs. You could walk in and start straightaway. But nothing paid a lot.

I've been trying to think hard but it's nearly half a century ago. I think we earned about £4 or £5 a week. Certainly no more than that – even if that.

I do remember a room was £3 or £3 10s per week and I had to make enough tips to live. Working in coffee bars was the most fun but not a lot of tips, so if you worked in a restaurant you got more, plus sometimes something to eat.

We were mad – very rarely buying food; you needed half a crown for a frothy coffee and one cup lasted hours.

In comparison a bag of chips was probably about sixpence. I do remember I paid just over a £1 per week to get my hair set at "Herbies" next door to the cinema that was showing *South Pacific* in Tottenham Court Road.

I would have a huge blonde beehive that was solid. Then I'd spend five shillings half way through the week for a "comb out" when it was taken down and brushed out then put back up again and re-lacquered. You had to have that done or it itched like hell. The appointments were regular bookings which were kept no matter what else you went without or how many layers of newspapers went into your shoes. There were no charity shops then, and of course, you had to look good to work.

So another week you could not pay the rent – no rent books or any protection so that was it. Rent due today – can't pay – out you go.

Then you'd meet up with a crowd and someone who had paid their rent would sneak you into their room which was good of them. If their landlord had seen what was going on they would have been out as well.

If you were all in the same boat it was on to the Circle Line for a couple of hours' sleep until you were spotted and turfed off.

I think that it was what I remember – the friendship – we were all skint but if you shared and looked out for each other you survived.

The miles we walked – most of the cheaper rooms were in Kentish Town or Holloway so when you at last went home from Soho, you walked.

There may have been late night buses but I can't remember.

Other haunts we used were The Heaven and Hell, The Zambezi in a basement and The Black and White café.

Sighting of famous people always added to the excitement. I remember Wee Willie Harris in his drape jacket, suede shoes and coloured hair.

Another regular was Ray Patterson, the obligatory "yank" who was in loads of films.

My only claim to fame at the time was to be in the 2 I's when the *New Musical Express* came to photograph the new juke box. It was either the first or the latest Wurlitzer in the country.

They had a Buddy Holly "lookalike" singer and decided they needed a little "glamour" added. The manager, Tom I think his name was, said "Come on, Chris, you're what we need". The funny thing was I'd bought some cheap material and hand-stitched it into a couple of shift dresses and that's what I was wearing.

I know it was either the second or third week in October 1959 that the photos appeared because I went to a newsagent's close to my sister's home, ordered and paid for a copy and asked them to save it for me. But when I did go back several weeks later they hadn't got it so I never got to keep a copy.

Then it was all over. Sometime in the 1960s I must have grown up at last, went to live with my sister and got a proper job and the mad exciting thing was all over.

I suppose this is all pathetic by today's standards but I wouldn't have missed it for the world.

On rare occasions it all comes back to me and I still experience the euphoria of that time – not sure it's good for the blood pressure though.'

The Heaven and Hell hostess club had started life as a Beatnik club. It was just across the road and a few doors down from the 2 I's on the corner of Old Compton Street and Dean Street.

I Hadn't a Clue

'I hadn't a clue what was going on'
Eric Nugent

Other things don't change either. For example, names people adopted or had given to them.

If someone has the nickname 'Rockin' you think of someone new to the scene.

Well, how about Rockin' Ricky, alias Eric Nugent – who was on the scene in the late fifties – and still called Rockin' Ricky today.

Eric recalls:

'The first time Tom Littlewood gave me a job at the I's he got me serving coffee.

I hadn't a clue what was going on at the time – I had just come out of the army. The first person I served coffee to was Wee Willie Harris – unforgettable. But for me Terry Dene is the most memorable but there was so much going on there – you just couldn't take it all in.

One particular guy I remember was Keith Kelly – he played there and had a hit record. Unfortunately, he had a bad car accident and had to leave the business. I think he now lives on Jersey.

Later I went back to Manchester and that's where it started for me.

I formed my own band, The Velvet Collars. In 1976 we got into the Guinness Book of Records for playing rock 'n' roll for 144 hours non-stop.

I recorded two songs in 1977, which became successful for me in 1978 in Europe; they were "Someone Someone" and "Sheila".

That band split round about 1982 then I formed another band called Ricky and the Rebounds and we did extensive tours all over Europe.

I don't do so much on the road now, only recording.'

Keith Kelly had been the vocalist/rhythm guitarist with the John Barry Seven, from York, and had a hit record called 'Tease Me' in about 1960.

Keith had a great vocal style, played excellent guitar, and was superb on the chromatic harmonica, rather like Larry Adler.

Sleeping Rough

'*Sleeping rough was quite an adventure*'
Peter Mole

Southend-based group Chris and the Confederates, a five piece band comprising guitar, piano, drums, bass and a singer, had been gigging around Essex for a couple of years, and were at the stage of wanting to 'go pro'.

Peter Mole remembers:

'The chance came when we were offered an audition to play a five night a week gig at the famous 2 I's Coffee Bar in London's West End.

We arrived and met the owner, Tom Littlewood, a canny guy who actually charged us an admission fee to the club to do the audition! We passed and were offered the princely sum of £4 per night between us.

The problem was that by accepting, it would mean that the existing resident group, a four piece outfit from Birmingham, would be out of work. After a pint or three with our new found friends from Brum, it was decided to share the gig, thereby giving us about nine shillings [approx 45pence] each per day! However, with two lead guitars, piano, sax, two bass guitars, two drummers and a singer, we anticipated some great sessions.

For those who have never visited the I's, the live music happened downstairs in the cellar, which was no bigger than a large room.

The punters paid a fee upstairs in the coffee bar and came downstairs to watch the band but had to go back up for a drink or something to eat. No alcohol was served.

Having agreed to work for next to nothing, our main problem was accommodation, or at least the lack of it. Still we had youth on our side and sleeping rough was quite an adventure to us; Hammersmith Flyover,

Charing Cross Bridge, various underground stations and even the Brummie group van if we could walk as far as Battersea where for some reason it was permanently parked!

Some of us occasionally managed to persuade a local to let us kip on their floor. Food was another issue, but with careful management and the generosity of some of the cafés, particularly The Pollo Bar at the end of Old Compton Street, we survived. We even managed a half ounce of Old Holborn and a couple packets of greens – cigarette papers – per day. But the music was great.

On most nights the I's was buzzing, full to bursting and the guys in the extended group were getting increasingly frustrated at the pittance we were earning. It was suggested that one of us should approach Tom and demand more money, and I got the short straw.

Feeling a bit like Oliver Twist I had a long in-depth discussion with Tom, and after at least thirty seconds it was clear that my quest was in vain. However as if to prove that he really did have a heart, as I turned to go, Tom called me back and in his inimitable Northern accent said "Eh drummer, 'ave an 'am roll."

The gig lasted several weeks until we were offered a two-month gig at a club in Germany, but that is another story!

However, I will always remember with great fondness those crazy few weeks. We never stopped laughing, had some great sessions and met some fantastic people.'

The Pollo Bar is still there and often finds its way onto the 'top cheap London eats' lists. It is an Italian restaurant, but not fancy. The inside looks something like a truckers' café, with Formica tables and little booths; and there is more room downstairs if it looks full. There isn't a lot of space and the tables are packed in, but the food is good.

What the Public Wanted

'*They didn't know what the public wanted*'
Terry Wayne

'If you want to get in trouble
let me tell you how to do it.
Get yourself a guitar
then you're right into it.'

The opening lines from 'Talking Guitar Blues' brings me to Tin Pan Alley. After all, you needed to buy an instrument and the Alley was the place.

Terry Wayne remembers it well.

'We used to meet at Charing Cross Road – at that time there were a lot of musos running around in the alley.

I think it was a place called Salmas who had the first American guitars over here. We saw a Gibson I remember – similar to the one Carl Perkins used – it was a beautiful "Switchmaster". We just had to look at it and dream.

Then The Fenders arrived – but that was later on.

There was a shop on the corner and I remember all the guys used to come in on their way to a gig.

One day the Rolling Stones came in – this was in the early sixties – they had a van – saying can I try this guitar or that one. They were turning the place upside down and not giving a damn about anybody or anything – or the way they looked.

Tin Pan Alley was full of songwriters and song sellers and they sang all the time. It really opened up the scene.

I managed to get the names of the American publishers and then go to their subsidiaries over here – and say – can I have this song? This was in the early days around 1956 or 1957.

The English publishers really did not know what they had. They were sitting on stuff and until somebody woke them up – you know put a bomb under their feet – they didn't know what the public wanted.

I got a lot of work touring the American bases over here – but Soho was really the home of music at that time.

I was auditioning for a gig with my father – we did rock-a-billy stuff – so went to this guys office just around the corner from the 2 I's. In we went and did our stuff and the manager came round his name was Bill Sawyer I think – and said, "Well, we want the boy but not his dad".

So that was it. He stepped down and I got a five-year contract. They "groomed" me and got me ready for the business – it gave me good presentation education.

So I started touring all the dance halls – which then got me onto the *Six-Five Special* with the Vernon Girls. That was around 1957–58, which then led onto a recording contract. It's funny how things in life turn out.

A bit later I went to Sweden. The Grade organization had the "rights" to Cliff Richard and there was a company in Sweden called Tellstar Productions who wanted Cliff but he was busy elsewhere so I went instead. I did a two-week tour and because it went so well they wanted to keep me there.'

Terry actually had the first self-penned rock 'n' roll record in the UK. All other acts at that time covered US hits. His song 'Slim Jim Tie' was voted the most iconic song of any fashion.

In 2007 Terry Wayne was nominated for membership of the Rockabilly Hall Of Fame, and is the only UK act to receive this honour.

He had been retired from the music scene for many years but made his comeback at the 2 I's reunion gig organized by *Tales From The Woods* in January 2007.

The Vernons Girls were originally a choir that was put together as part of the social activities of Vernon's Pools, the Liverpool-based football pool company.

However, they became so accomplished and sought after that the company set them up professionally in the expectation that they would bring publicity to Vernon's.

The Vernons Girls' big break came when Jack Good decided that they were what he needed for his seminal rock 'n' roll show *Six-Five Special*. As this was a BBC show and advertising was prohibited, they were fortunate that their association with the pools' company did not stand in the way.

There were sixteen girls in all with one or two extras standing in the wings as back-up.

The group were an immediate success and brought a much needed feminine balance to the TV programme. They went on to do all Jack Good's early musical shows, transferring with him to independent television for *Oh Boy!* and *Boy Meets Girl*.

In addition to work on concert tours, they were also in great demand as backing singers for many of the stars of the day and appeared on many more records than is apparent from their modest discography.

Tales From The Woods is an unconventional Roots Music magazine published several times a year and encompassing 1950s style rock'n'roll, Rock-a-Billy, Country, Blues, Soul, Jazz, Reggae, etc.

It includes gig information, reviews of shows and record/CD releases, obituaries of artists who have recently died, etc.

The magazine also includes satire, political comment, comedy and generally has an irreverent approach.

The only rules are nothing libellous or slanderous, and avoid deeply insulting personal attacks on individuals.

Light-hearted satirical comments on well known celebrities and politicians, however, are welcome.

Atmosphere is not Around Today

'It's a pity the same atmosphere is not around today'
John Harris and Gordon Fleming

The early 1960s saw the beginning of a change in the music scene and, with the coming of The Beatles and The Cavern in Liverpool, places like the 2 I's began to lose their influence.

Like me John Harris was a fan and 'punter of the club scene' in his teens and remembers the 2 I's:

'It was always very busy. I used to go for a coffee sometimes in my lunch hour. I was about seventeen at the time and I remember in the evening it was a very glamorous place – lots of bright lights. As you walked passed you could hear the music from the cellar – and there were always crowds around the place trying get in.

Later, as I grew up we started going to other clubs and the scene began to change and the 2 I's lost the top position.'

His old school friend Gordon Fleming talked of

'Soho at the time was an exciting place to be, although I was slightly later getting into the club scene. But there is no doubt the I's had it, partly I think because of its location. It was in the high street of Soho.

Things began to change in the early 1960s with the "mods and rockers" thing, and other clubs came to prominence.'

Pauline Webber who was also more attuned to Soho in the mid sixties used to 'haunt' the Macabre coffee house where the tables were coffin shaped.

'I remember this guy called Iron Jack who used to hang around. He was on a bus one night when I was going home with my boyfriend. All of a sudden this guy came reaching down the back of my seat shouting "Anglo saxon whore", "anglo saxon prostitute".

He gained the name because he wore a large steel boot – one leg being shorter than the other. He was a true eccentric and walked around the area wearing a long black cloak and a rather large homburg style hat. Apparently, he had had a very "colourful" life and talked about things on the fringes of life – the occult, fortune telling and so forth.

Jack used to play Banjo with someone called Gypsy Larry who played guitar. Larry, apparently, was the leader of their little gang. Gypsy Larry eventually became the doorman at Ronnie Scott's club.

Suddenly he stopped and got off at the next stop. Sometime later I saw his picture in a book – he was the local Soho lunatic I think.

I had a flat in Chelsea at the time and decided I needed extra money because I wanted to travel, so I got a job in the Piccadilly Theatre – that was fun – it was *Man of La Mancha* a wonderful show. I only planned to stay six months but, because it was such a good show, I ended up staying more than a year.

I remember another incident. There was an old lady who travelled on the bus without paying. One night there was a Pakistani bus conductor who asked her for her fare. She refused saying she had no money and he started to argue. Someone else on the bus shouted "Don't pick on her you bloody paki." Remember this was the early 1960s. It reminds me that even then there was an anti-immigrant feeling.

When I was seventeen I was walking along Old Compton Street and I saw the street in front of me and I remember thinking "I can't walk down there". It was Frith Street – there was something horrible down there and sometime later I discovered that that's where my ancestors lived. It took me years to find out.'

The Le Macabre coffee bar just off Wardour Street had coffin-shaped tables, and was the centre of the Beatnik culture in London during the early fifties.

I certainly can remember it with some affection.

Gordon continued,

'In 1961–2 the Top Ten in Carnaby Street was busy and we used to go and see Cyril Davies play there. I remember some of Screaming Lord Sutch's "savages" used to come down.

I also saw Christine Keeler there. They were great times as a young man – it is a pity the same atmosphere is not around today.'

Christine Keeler is best known for her involvement with the then Secretary of State for War, John Profumo. However, she was no stranger to Soho.

When she was fifteen, she found work as a model at a dress shop in London's Soho quarter and at seventeen, had a baby after an affair with an African-American sergeant from Lakenheath Air Force base.

She initially worked as a waitress at a restaurant on Baker Street and there met Maureen O'Connor, a girl who worked at Murray's Cabaret Club in Soho. She introduced Keeler to the owner, Percy Murray, who hired her almost immediately as a topless showgirl. While at Murray's she met Dr. Stephen Ward.

Soon the two were living together with the outward appearance of being a couple, but, according to her, it was a platonic 'brother and sister'-type relationship.

In July of 1961, she was introduced to John Profumo.

Profumo entered into an affair with Keeler, not realizing that she was also sleeping with Yevgeny Ivanov, a naval attaché at the embassy of the Soviet Union.

The affair was terminated by the government's Cabinet Secretary, Sir Norman Brook, who spoke to Profumo on the advice of Sir Roger Hollis, the head of MI5. On 9th August 1961, Profumo wrote to Keeler advising her he could no longer see her.

Murray's Cabaret Club in Beak Street opened in 1933. Based on an American speak-easy joint those who joined were assured that their names would not be disclosed.

As a result the club was regularly visited by the rich and famous including members of the royal family, who rubbed shoulders with the likes of the Kray brothers. Princess Margaret was a known regular.

It was famous for the floor shows with attractive girls wearing very little.

Over a relatively few years the area became alive with a variety of interesting venues.

If Frith Street is the centre of Italian culture in London then Bar Italia is the Vatican.

Over the years it became the most well established and famous Italian coffee bar for may people. The walls were originally covered in boxing photos.

A small coffee bar, apparently unchanged in years, it simply oozes Latin charm. At any time of the night, you'll have to queue for a coffee and there will be no room inside to drink it.

Bar Italia is an institution in Soho and being one of the only places you can go at any time of the day or night, it certainly has its benefits.

The Coach & Horses pub in Greek Street established itself as the home of the 'Private Eye's lunches'.

It is a great old Sohoites pub and so different from all the others around; notable for its customers past and present as much as anything.

The days when the likes of John Hurt and Peter O'Toole rested their feet on the urinal-like trough at the foot of the bar are gone, but the Coach still attracts recognizable faces; even mine!

It was also the favourite watering-hole of Jeffrey Bernard and the setting of the play *Jeffrey Bernard is Unwell*.

Down a small side street linking Shaftesbury Avenue to Gerrard Street in China Town, De Hems pub is unsurprisingly, if you know any of the language, Dutch.

It was apparently taken over by a Dutch sailor in the early part of the twentieth century and was home to the Dutch resistance during the Second World War.

Being Dutch you wouldn't expect anything less than the friendliest of services and the staff all keep to the tradition splendidly. De Hems is a bit of a mecca for the Dutch in London, especially if their national team is playing football.

In 1953 the Italian actress Gina Lollobrigida opened the Moka coffee bar at 29 Frith Street in Soho, which provided London with its first Gaggia expresso coffee machine. So popular was the drink that for a while Frith Street was known as 'froth street'.

It could be argued that the simple opening of this West End coffee bar was the early morning double expresso that London needed to kick-start its way out of the grey post-war depression, setting itself up to become the world's trendiest city in only a decade's time.

The Roundhouse was important and hosted Cyril Davies and Alexis Korner who started the first Blues and Barrelhouse club, having regular sessions on a Thursday night. Sonny Terry and Brownie McGhee were guests and it was, in fact, Brownie who played electric guitar there. It was quite an innovation then.

The Scene in Ham Yard just off Great Windmill Street became important as one of the early HQs for the mod scene in early 1960s. It was owned by Ronan O'Rahally, who later founded Radio Caroline.

The club's decor didn't match the smart cut of their clothes, being a bizarre dingy basement catacomb where the walls were padded and the floor was littered with cushions. It was ideal for the lifestyle they led, where you were buzzing into the early hours of the morning and needed a club that stayed open as late as 5 a.m. on a Sunday.

It's funny how some things never change. Today we are often moaning about what 'developers' want to do in our area. Well, it was just the same in Soho in 1962.

The developers had been nosing around the area with an eye on modernizing and expanding. For generations the area had been a maze of little streets and alleyways.

During the great Victorian era Soho remained virtually unchanged.

The area known as Soho was in many ways a village community within the great metropolis. One of the main streets was Berwick Street with the market – still vibrant today – and Soho Square the meeting place and green – again still the same today.

Each street had its own 'function'. The film world had most of Wardour Street with Archer Street 'belonging' to the theatre and to the actors and actresses.

In 1960 the 'working' girls were taken off the streets but then the phone boxes became their 'shop window'. Then suddenly a very tall building grew adjacent to Berwick Street market.

It was a panic measure to rehouse people from slums. However, this was not the developers directly, it was Westminster Council. And they were planning to build more tower blocks over the next few years. The council did plead that they were hoping to maintain the uniqueness of Soho.

Many council officials were of the opinion that they and not the developers should stay in control. They argued that if the area was preserved, quite likely in the future it would be possible to enjoy a pedestrianized area running from Oxford Street down to Piccadilly Circus.

Well, with congestion charges it is heading that way.

Of course, coffee bars were only part of the scene. Many restaurants opened up in the area in a very few years and it has to be said that hygiene was not always top of the list.

A survey was carried out in late 1960 early 1961 and it was found that tuberculosis was over four times more common in the catering trade in Soho as in the general population, and certainly far more common than in catering across the country.

It was a Dr. Nash the medical director of the south-west London mass x-ray service who stated that a waiter who carried the disease and who coughed in the stuffy atmosphere was liable to give 'quite a good dose' of infection to the person he was serving!

Inevitably the question of one's resistance to the disease was important.

In general it was thought that anyone over twenty-five years old was probably less vulnerable because of natural resistance gained in their life.

In a way those days have gone – and I don't just mean the date has changed.

In the early sixties things began to change and the 2 I's lost its place at the top list of coffee bars.

In 1963 the classic line-up of the Rolling Stones – including Bill Wyman on bass and Charlie Watts on drums – made their first-ever live appearance, at the Flamingo Club in Soho.

Georgie Fame had a residency for three years at the infamous Flamingo Club.

Affectionately known as the Mingo, the doorway was just south of Shaftesbury Avenue on the west side of Wardour Street. It was a basement, dark and atmospheric. There was a bar, a small dance floor and the stage.

In July of that year The Pickwick Club opened in Great Newport Street and quickly becomes a favourite with London's swinging 'in-crowd', which included The Beatles.

The Ad-Lib club was launched by Club owners Nicholas Luard and Chelsea set member Lord Timothy Willoughby.

Later in the year it was re-launched by new owners Al and Bob Burnett, with Brian Morris of posh Mayfair. It would swiftly become the trendiest club in London, frequented by The Beatles, The Rolling Stones and numerous other leading lights of London's fast set.

On New Year's Eve, the Kinks got their first big break, playing a gig at the China Garden restaurant in Soho, impressing booking agent Arthur Howe who signed them as a support act on a Dave Clark Five tour, starting the following day.

After 1963, many restrictions were eased on exchange of artists with USA, therefore many clubs prospered after that period.

In early 1964 The Marquee Club opened up a new venue in Wardour Street. The leading group on the opening night was the Yardbirds, featuring their new guitarist, Eric Clapton. The gig was recorded and released as the UK R&B classic, 'Five Live Yardbirds'.

New management took control of and relaunched the Piccadilly Club as the Scene Club, under which name it went on to achieve legendary status among Britain's mods. Then in August, The Who began an epochal series of Wednesday night gigs at the Scene Club.

In December an unknown American folk duo Simon & Garfunkel made their UK debut at The Flamingo Club in Soho.

On to 1965 and Ronnie Scott moved his jazz club from Gerrard Street and reopened it in Frith Street. After he relocated the club he put on jazz six nights week with names such as Count Basie, Sarah Vaughan, Ella Fitzgerald appearing there.

In November, The Jimi Hendrix Experience marked its debut at a press reception at the Bag O'Nails club.

The Bag O'Nails club was in Kingly Street and was a meeting point for musicians in the 1960s.

It was one of the favourite venues for The Beatles.

Ronnie Scott's was also the last venue played by Jimi Hendrix in September 1970; just days later he died.

Towards the end of 1965 Elton John started work as a tea-boy at Mills Music in Denmark Street.

In early 1966 the Ad Lib club burned down and London's swinging scene moved to the Scotch of St. James, the Speakeasy and the Cromwellian.

So Soho can justifiably claim its place in the history of music and cultural development in post-war London. Those of us who knew and enjoyed those days really do have some wonderful memories.

Working in theatres in London I am still a frequent visitor to the area. Yes, it has changed but still retains a unique charm and atmosphere.

Epilogue

Rockin' Gerry Champion penned the following verse for the unveiling of the plaque. It seems to sum it up nicely.

Paul Lincoln and Tom Littlewood
soon to be renowned
decided to run a coffee bar
which was soon to Rock Soho town.
From 1956 when in Tommy Steele was groovin'
the 2 I's was the joint to get you movin'.
From miles around musicians came
both instrumental and vocal,
entertaining those who packed in each night
both sightseers and local.
The Vipers were the favourites
with their own brand of skiffle,
Their followers one and all agreed
all other music's piffle.
Then USA's Haley and Elvis
Gene, Jerry and Eddy,
Richard, Buddy and the Big Bopper
Soon changed the scene to rock 'n' roll
And skiffle came a cropper.
The 2 I's welcomed one and all
to come and show their talent
new names and idols topped the bill
names all true rockers know.
Wee Willie Harris, Terry Dene, Marty Wilde
Danny Rivers too, Cliff Richard, Rory
Blackwell, Vince Eager, Vince Taylor,

Keith Kelly – to name but a few.
Not forgetting the great Dave 'Lord' Sutch
and his raving savages too.
Many more graced the 2 I's stage
Some good, some in between,
was this to be their rise to fame
or just a teenage dream.
The 2 I's days alas have passed
and all that's left is the ghost
of times when rock 'n' roll was king
and the 2 I's was its host.

Gerry Champion
18th September 2006

Index

Page references in **bold** indicate where the personal memories of contributers can be found.